GRADIENT-BASED BLOCK MATCHING MOTION ESTIMATION AND OBJECT TRACKING WITH PYTHON AND TKINTER

VIVIAN SIAHAAN
RISMON HASIHOLAN SIANIPAR

Copyright © 2024 BALIGE Publishing

All rights reserved. No part of this book may be reproduced, stored in a retrieval system, or transmitted in any form or by any means, without the prior written permission of the publisher, except in the case of brief quotations embedded in critical articles or reviews. Every effort has been made in the preparation of this book to ensure the accuracy of the information presented. However, the information contained in this book is sold without warranty, either express or implied. Neither the authors, nor BALIGE Publishing or its dealers and distributors, will be held liable for any damages caused or alleged to have been caused directly or indirectly by this book. BALIGE Publishing has endeavored to provide trademark information about all of the companies and products mentioned in this book by the appropriate use of capitals. However, BALIGE Publishing cannot guarantee the accuracy of this information.

Published: APRIL 2024
Production reference: 0400424
Published by BALIGE Publishing Ltd.
BALIGE, North Sumatera

ABOUT THE AUTHOR

Vivian Siahaan is a highly motivated individual with a passion for continuous learning and exploring new areas. Born and raised in Hinalang Bagasan, Balige, situated on the picturesque banks of Lake Toba, she completed her high school education at SMAN 1 Balige. Vivian's journey into the world of programming began with a deep dive into various languages such as Java, Android, JavaScript, CSS, C++, Python, R, Visual Basic, Visual C#, MATLAB, Mathematica, PHP, JSP, MySQL, SQL Server, Oracle, Access, and more. Starting from scratch, Vivian diligently studied programming, focusing on mastering the fundamental syntax and logic. She honed her skills by creating practical GUI applications, gradually building her expertise. One particular area of interest for Vivian is animation and game development, where she aspires to make significant contributions. Alongside her programming and mathematical pursuits, she also finds joy in indulging in novels, nurturing her love for literature. Vivian Siahaan's passion for programming and her extensive knowledge are reflected in the numerous ebooks she has authored. Her works, published by Sparta Publisher, cover a wide range of topics, including "Data Structure with Java," "Java Programming: Cookbook," "C++ Programming: Cookbook," "C Programming For High Schools/Vocational Schools and Students," "Java Programming for SMA/SMK," "Java Tutorial: GUI, Graphics and Animation," "Visual Basic Programming: From A to Z," "Java Programming for Animation and Games," "C# Programming for SMA/SMK and Students," "MATLAB For Students and Researchers," "Graphics in JavaScript: Quick Learning Series," "JavaScript Image Processing Methods: From A to Z," "Java GUI Case Study: AWT & Swing," "Basic CSS and JavaScript," "PHP/MySQL Programming: Cookbook," "Visual Basic: Cookbook," "C++ Programming for High Schools/Vocational Schools and Students," "Concepts and Practices of C++," "PHP/MySQL For Students," "C# Programming: From A to Z," "Visual Basic for SMA/SMK and Students," and "C# .NET and SQL Server for High School/Vocational School and Students." Furthermore, at the ANDI Yogyakarta publisher, Vivian Siahaan has contributed to several notable books, including "Python Programming Theory and Practice," "Python GUI Programming," "Python GUI and Database," "Build From Zero School Database Management System In Python/MySQL," "Database Management System in Python/MySQL," "Python/MySQL For Management Systems of Criminal Track Record Database," "Java/MySQL For Management Systems of Criminal Track Records Database," "Database and Cryptography Using Java/MySQL," and "Build From Zero School Database Management System With Java/MySQL." Vivian's diverse range of expertise in programming languages, combined with her passion for exploring new horizons, makes her a dynamic and versatile individual in the field of technology. Her dedication to learning, coupled with her strong analytical and problem-solving skills, positions her as a valuable asset in any programming endeavor. Vivian Siahaan's contributions to the world of programming and literature continue to inspire and empower aspiring programmers and readers alike.

Rismon Hasiholan Sianipar, born in Pematang Siantar in 1994, is a distinguished researcher and expert in the field of electrical engineering. After completing his education at SMAN 3 Pematang Siantar, Rismon ventured to the city of Jogjakarta to pursue his academic journey. He obtained his Bachelor of Engineering (S.T) and Master of Engineering (M.T) degrees in Electrical Engineering from Gadjah Mada University in 1998 and 2001, respectively, under the guidance of esteemed professors, Dr. Adhi Soesanto and Dr. Thomas Sri Widodo. During his studies, Rismon focused on researching non-stationary signals and their energy analysis using time-frequency maps. He explored the dynamic nature of signal energy distribution on time-frequency maps and developed innovative techniques using discrete wavelet transformations to design non-linear filters for data pattern analysis. His research showcased the application of these techniques in various fields. In recognition of his academic prowess, Rismon was awarded the prestigious Monbukagakusho scholarship by the Japanese Government in 2003. He went on to pursue his Master of Engineering (M.Eng) and Doctor of Engineering (Dr.Eng) degrees at Yamaguchi University, supervised by Prof. Dr. Hidetoshi Miike. Rismon's master's and doctoral theses revolved around combining the SR-FHN (Stochastic Resonance Fitzhugh-Nagumo) filter strength with the cryptosystem ECC (elliptic curve cryptography) 4096-bit. This innovative approach effectively suppressed noise in digital images and videos while ensuring their authenticity. Rismon's research findings have been published in renowned international scientific journals, and his patents have been officially registered in Japan. Notably, one of his patents, with registration number 2008-009549, gained recognition. He actively collaborates with several universities and research institutions in Japan, specializing in cryptography, cryptanalysis, and digital forensics, particularly in the areas of audio, image, and video analysis. With a passion for knowledge sharing, Rismon has authored numerous national and international scientific articles and authored several national books. He has also actively participated in workshops related to cryptography, cryptanalysis, digital watermarking, and digital forensics. During these workshops, Rismon has assisted Prof. Hidetoshi Miike in developing applications related to digital image and video processing, steganography, cryptography, watermarking, and more, which serve as valuable training materials. Rismon's field of interest encompasses multimedia security, signal processing, digital image and video analysis, cryptography, digital communication, digital forensics, and data compression. He continues to advance his research by developing applications using programming languages such as Python, MATLAB, C++, C, VB.NET, C#.NET, R, and Java. These applications serve both research and commercial purposes, further contributing to the advancement of signal and image analysis. Rismon Hasiholan Sianipar is a dedicated researcher and expert in the field of electrical engineering, particularly in the areas of signal processing, cryptography, and digital forensics. His academic achievements, patented inventions, and extensive publications demonstrate his commitment to advancing knowledge in these fields. Rismon's contributions to academia and his collaborations with prestigious institutions in Japan have solidified his position as a respected figure in the scientific community. Through his ongoing research and development of innovative applications, Rismon continues to make significant contributions to the field of electrical engineering.

ABOUT THE BOOK

The first project, gui_motion_analysis_gbbm.py, is designed to streamline motion analysis in videos using the Gradient-Based Block Matching Algorithm (GBBM) alongside a user-friendly Graphical User Interface (GUI). It encompasses various objectives, including intuitive GUI design with Tkinter, enabling video playback control, performing optical flow analysis, and allowing parameter configuration for tailored motion analysis. The GUI also facilitates interactive zooming, frame-wise analysis, and offers visual feedback through motion vector overlays. Robust error handling and multi-instance support enhance stability and usability, while dynamic title updates provide context within the interface. Overall, the project empowers users with a versatile tool for comprehensive motion analysis in videos.

By integrating the GBBM algorithm with an intuitive GUI, gui_motion_analysis_gbbm.py simplifies motion analysis in videos. Its objectives range from GUI design to parameter configuration, enabling users to control video playback, perform optical flow analysis, and visualize motion patterns effectively. With features like interactive zooming, frame-wise analysis, and visual feedback, users can delve into motion dynamics seamlessly. Robust error handling ensures stability, while multi-instance support allows for concurrent analysis. Dynamic title updates enhance user awareness, culminating in a versatile tool for in-depth motion analysis.

The second project, gui_motion_analysis_gbbm_pyramid.py, is dedicated to offering an accessible interface for video motion analysis, employing the Gradient-Based Block Matching Algorithm (GBBM) with a Pyramid Approach. Its objectives encompass several crucial aspects.

Primarily, the project responds to the demand for motion analysis in video processing across diverse domains like computer vision and robotics. By integrating the GBBM algorithm into a GUI, it democratizes motion analysis, catering to users without specialized programming or computer vision skills. Leveraging the GBBM algorithm's effectiveness, particularly with the Pyramid Approach, enhances performance and robustness, enabling accurate motion estimation across various scales. The GUI offers extensive control options and visualization features, empowering users to customize analysis parameters and inspect motion dynamics comprehensively. Overall, this project endeavors to advance video processing and analysis by providing an intuitive interface backed by cutting-edge algorithms, fostering accessibility and efficiency in motion analysis tasks.

The third project, gui_motion_analysis_gbbm_adaptive.py, introduces a GUI application for video motion estimation, employing the Gradient-Based Block Matching Algorithm (GBBM) with Adaptive Block Size. Users can interact with video files, control playback, navigate frames, and visualize optical flow between consecutive frames, facilitated by features like zooming and panning. Developed with Tkinter in Python, the GUI provides intuitive controls for adjusting motion estimation parameters and playback options upon launch.

At its core, the application dynamically adjusts block sizes based on local gradient magnitude, enhancing motion estimation accuracy, especially in areas with varying complexity. Utilizing PIL and OpenCV libraries, it handles image processing tasks and video file operations, enabling users to interact with the video display canvas for enhanced analysis. Overall, gui_motion_analysis_gbbm_adaptive.py offers a versatile solution for motion analysis in videos, empowering users with visualization tools and parameter customization for diverse applications like video compression and object tracking.

The fourth project, gui_motion_analysis_gbbm_lucas_kanade.py, introduces a GUI for motion estimation in videos, incorporating both the Gradient-Based Block Matching Algorithm (GBBM) and Lucas-Kanade Optical Flow. It begins by importing necessary libraries such as tkinter for GUI development, PIL for image processing, imageio for video file handling, cv2 for computer vision operations, and numpy for numerical computation. The VideoGBBM_LK_OpticalFlow class serves as the application container, initializing attributes and defining methods for video loading, playback control, parameter setting, frame display, and optical flow visualization. With features like zooming, panning, and event handling for user interactions, the script offers a comprehensive tool for visualizing and analyzing motion dynamics in videos using two distinct optical flow estimation techniques.

The fifth project, gui_motion_analysis_gbbm_sift.py, introduces a GUI application for optical flow analysis in videos, employing both the Gradient-Based Block Matching Algorithm (GBBM) and Scale-Invariant Feature Transform (SIFT). It begins by importing essential libraries such as tkinter for GUI development, PIL for image processing, imageio for video handling, and OpenCV for computer vision tasks like optical flow computation. The VideoGBBM_SIFT_OpticalFlow class orchestrates the application, initializing GUI elements and defining methods for video loading, playback control, frame display, and optical flow computation using both GBBM and SIFT algorithms. With features for parameter adjustment, frame navigation, zooming, and event handling for user interactions, the script offers a user-friendly interface for in-depth optical flow analysis, enabling insights into motion patterns and dynamics within videos.

The sixth project, gui_motion_analysis_gbbm_orb.py script, offers a user-friendly interface for motion estimation in videos, utilizing both the Gradient-Based Block Matching Algorithm (GBBM) and ORB (Oriented FAST and Rotated BRIEF) optical flow techniques. Its primary goal is to enable users to analyze and visualize motion dynamics within video files effortlessly. The GUI application provides functionalities for opening video files, navigating frames, adjusting parameters like zoom scale and step size, and controlling playback with buttons for play, pause, stop, next frame, and previous frame.

Key to the application's functionality is its ability to compute and visualize optical flow using both GBBM and ORB algorithms. Optical flow, depicting object motion in videos, is represented with vectors overlaid on video frames, aiding users in understanding motion patterns and dynamics. Interactive features such as mouse wheel zooming and dragging enhance user exploration of video frames and optical flow visualizations, allowing dynamic adjustment of viewing perspective to focus on specific regions or analyze motion at different scales. Overall, this project provides a comprehensive tool for video motion analysis, merging user-friendly interface elements with advanced motion estimation techniques to empower users in tasks ranging from surveillance to computer vision research.

The seventh project showcases object tracking using the Gradient-Based Block Matching Algorithm (GBBM), vital in various computer vision applications like surveillance and robotics. By continuously locating and tracking objects of interest in video streams, it highlights GBBM's practical application for real-time tracking. The GUI interface simplifies interaction with video files, allowing easy opening and visualization of frames. Users control playback, navigate frames, and adjust zoom scale, while the heart of the project lies in GBBM's implementation for tracking objects. GBBM estimates object motion by comparing pixel blocks between consecutive frames, generating motion vectors that describe the object's movement. Users can select regions of interest for tracking, adjust algorithm parameters, and receive visual feedback through dynamically adjusting bounding boxes around tracked objects, making it an educational tool for experimenting with object tracking techniques within an accessible interface.

The eight project endeavors to create an application for object tracking using the Gradient-Based Block Matching Algorithm (GBBM) with a Pyramid Approach, catering to various computer vision applications like surveillance and autonomous vehicles. Built with Tkinter in Python, the user-friendly interface presents controls for video display, object tracking, and parameter adjustment upon launch. Users can load video files, play, pause, navigate frames, and adjust zoom levels effortlessly.

Central to the application is the GBBM algorithm with a pyramid approach for robust object tracking. By refining search spaces at multiple resolutions, it efficiently estimates motion vectors, accommodating scale variations and occlusions. The application visualizes tracked objects with bounding boxes on the video canvas and updates object coordinates dynamically, providing users with insights into object movement. Advanced features, including dynamic parameter adjustment, enhance the algorithm's adaptability, enabling users to fine-tune tracking based on video characteristics and requirements. Overall, this project offers a practical implementation of object tracking within an accessible interface, catering to users across expertise levels in computer vision.

The ninth project, "Object Tracking with Gradient-Based Block Matching Algorithm (GBBM) with Adaptive Block Size", focuses on developing a graphical user interface (GUI) application for object tracking in video files using computer vision techniques. Leveraging the GBBM algorithm, a prominent method for motion estimation, the project aims to enable efficient object tracking across video frames, enhancing user interaction and real-time monitoring capabilities.

The GUI interface facilitates seamless video file loading, playback control, frame navigation, and real-time object tracking, empowering users to interact with video frames, adjust zoom levels, and monitor tracked object coordinates throughout the video sequence. Central to the project's functionality is the adaptive block size variant of the GBBM algorithm, dynamically adjusting block sizes based on gradient magnitudes to improve tracking accuracy and robustness across various scenarios. By simplifying object tracking processes through intuitive GUI interactions, the project caters to users with limited programming expertise, fostering learning opportunities in computer vision and video processing. Additionally, the project serves as a platform for collaboration and experimentation, promoting knowledge sharing and innovation within the computer vision community while showcasing the practical applications of computer vision algorithms in surveillance, video analysis, and human-computer interaction domains.

The tenth project, "Object Tracking with SIFT Algorithm", introduces a GUI application developed with Python's tkinter library for tracking objects in videos using the Scale-Invariant Feature Transform (SIFT) algorithm. Upon launching, users access a window featuring video display, center coordinates of tracked objects, and control buttons. Supported video formats include mp4, avi, mkv, and wmv, with the "Open Video" button enabling file selection for display within the canvas widget.

Playback control buttons like "Play/Pause," "Stop," "Previous Frame," and "Next Frame" facilitate seamless navigation and video playback adjustments. A zoom combobox enhances user experience by allowing flexible zoom scaling. The SIFT algorithm facilitates object tracking by detecting and matching keypoints between frames, estimating motion vectors used to update the bounding box coordinates of the tracked object in real-time. Users can manually define object bounding boxes by clicking and dragging on the video canvas, offering both automated and manual tracking options for enhanced user control.

The eleventh project, "Object Tracking with ORB (Oriented FAST and Rotated BRIEF)", aims to develop a user-friendly GUI application for object tracking in videos using the ORB algorithm. Utilizing Python's Tkinter library, the project provides an interface where users can open video files of various formats and interact with playback and tracking functionalities. Users can control video playback, adjust zoom levels for detailed examination, and utilize the ORB algorithm for object detection and tracking.

The application integrates ORB for computing keypoints and descriptors across video frames, facilitating the estimation of motion vectors for object tracking. Real-time visualization of tracking progress through overlaid bounding boxes enhances user understanding, while interactive features like selecting regions of interest and monitoring bounding box coordinates provide further control and feedback. Overall, the "Object Tracking with ORB" project offers a comprehensive solution for video analysis tasks, combining intuitive controls, real-time visualization, and efficient tracking capabilities with the ORB algorithm.

CONTENT

MOTION ESTIMATION WITH GRADIENT-BASED BLOCK MATCHING ALGORITHM (GBBM)	**1**
DESCRIPTION	1
IMPORTING LIBRARIES	3
CLASS AND INITIALIZATION	4
CREATING WIDGETS	6
CONTROLLING VIDEO PLAYBACK	9
SHOWING FRAME	10
IMPLEMENTING GRADIENT BASED BLOCK MATCHING	12
SHOWING OPTICAL FLOW	16
HANDLING MOUSE EVENTS	19
NAVIGATING FRAME	21
SETTING WINDOW TITLE	22
RUNNING PROGRAM	23
SOURCE CODE	24
MOTION ESTIMATION WITH GRADIENT-BASED BLOCK MATCHING ALGORITHM (GBBM) WITH PYRAMID APPROACH	**33**
DESCRIPTION	33
IMPLEMENTING GRADIENT-BASED BLOCK MACHING WITH PYRAMID APPROACH	34
RUNNING PROGRAM	39
SOURCE CODE	40

MOTION ESTIMATION WITH GRADIENT-BASED BLOCK MATCHING ALGORITHM (GBBM) WITH ADAPTIVE BLOCK SIZE — 49

- DESCRIPTION — 49
- IMPLEMENTING GRADIENT-BASED BLOCK MACHING WITH ADAPTIVE BLOCK SIZE — 50
- RUNNING PROGRAM — 55
- SOURCE CODE — 55

COMBINING MOTION ESTIMATION WITH GRADIENT-BASED BLOCK MATCHING ALGORITHM (GBBM) AND LUCAS-KANADE — 56

- DESCRIPTION — 56
- IMPLEMENTING GRADIENT-BASED BLOCK MACHING AND LUCAS-KANADE — 65
- SHOWING OPTICAL FLOW — 67
- RUNNING PROGRAM — 70
- SOURCE CODE — 71

COMBINING MOTION ESTIMATION WITH GRADIENT-BASED BLOCK MATCHING ALGORITHM (GBBM) AND SIFT — 81

- DESCRIPTION — 81
- IMPLEMENTING SCALE-INVARIANT FEATURE TRANSFORM (SIFT) MOTION ESTIMATION — 83
- SHOWING OPTICAL FLOW FRAME — 86
- RUNNING PROGRAM — 87
- SOURCE CODE — 88

COMBINING MOTION ESTIMATION WITH GRADIENT-BASED BLOCK MATCHING ALGORITHM (GBBM) AND ORB — 99

- DESCRIPTION — 99
- IMPLEMENTING ORB (ORIENTED FAST AND ROTATED BRIEF) — 100
- SHOWING OPTICAL FLOW — 104
- RUNNING PROGRAM — 107
- SOURCE CODE — 108

OBJECT TRACKING WITH GRADIENT-BASED BLOCK MATCHING ALGORITHM (GBBM)   110

DESCRIPTION	110
CREATING WIDGETS	119
TRACKING OBJECT	122
UPDATING BOUNDING BOX RECTANGLE	125
SHOWING TRACKED OBJECT	126
RUNNING PROGRAM	129
SOURCE CODE	129

OBJECT TRACKING WITH GRADIENT-BASED BLOCK MATCHING ALGORITHM (GBBM) WITH PYRAMID APPORACH   137

DESCRIPTION	137
TRACKING OBJECT	138
RUNNING PROGRAM	142
SOURCE CODE	142

OBJECT TRACKING WITH GRADIENT-BASED BLOCK MATCHING ALGORITHM (GBBM) WITH ADAPTIVE BLOCK SIZE   151

DESCRIPTION	151
TRACKING OBJECT	153
RUNNING PROGRAM	157
SOURCE CODE	157

OBJECT TRACKING WITH SCALE-INVARIANT FEATURE TRANSFORM (SIFT)   166

DESCRIPTION	166
TRACKING OBJECT	167
RUNNING PROGRAM	171
SOURCE CODE	172

OBJECT TRACKING WITH ORB (ORIENTED FAST AND ROTATED BRIEF)   179

DESCRIPTION	179
TRACKING OBJECT	180
RUNNING PROGRAM	184
SOURCE CODE	185
Bibliography	**193**

MOTION ESTIMATION WITH GRADIENT-BASED BLOCK MATCHING ALGORITHM (GBBM)

DESCRIPTION

The purpose of the project encapsulated in the code, named gui_motion_analysis_gbbm.py, revolves around facilitating motion analysis in videos through the implementation of the Gradient-Based Block Matching Algorithm (GBBM) while providing a user-friendly Graphical User Interface (GUI) for interaction. Let's break down its objectives and functionality:

1. GUI Design and Layout: The project aims to provide an intuitive interface using Tkinter, a Python library for GUI development. The interface comprises various components such as buttons, entry fields, and canvases strategically organized to enhance user experience.
2. Video Playback and Control: The primary function is to enable users to load video files (in formats like mp4, avi, or mkv) and control their playback. Features include playing, pausing, stopping, and navigating through frames, empowering users to analyze motion at their desired pace.
3. Optical Flow Analysis: The core functionality revolves around performing optical flow analysis using the GBBM algorithm. Optical flow estimation is a crucial task

in computer vision, allowing the detection and tracking of motion patterns within consecutive frames of a video.
4. Parameter Configuration: Users can dynamically adjust parameters crucial for motion analysis, such as block size, search range, step size, and displacement (dx and dy), offering flexibility to tailor the analysis based on specific requirements or characteristics of the input video.
5. Interactive Zooming: The GUI facilitates zooming functionality, enabling users to magnify or shrink the displayed video frames and corresponding optical flow results. This feature enhances the visibility of motion patterns, especially in regions of interest within the video.
6. Frame-wise Analysis: The application supports frame-by-frame analysis, allowing users to scrutinize motion dynamics at a granular level. Users can navigate through frames sequentially or jump to specific time points within the video for detailed examination.
7. Visual Feedback: The project offers visual feedback by overlaying motion vectors onto the original video frames. This visualization aids in comprehending the direction and magnitude of motion between consecutive frames, aiding in qualitative and quantitative motion analysis.
8. Error Handling: Robust error handling mechanisms are implemented to ensure the stability and reliability of the application. Error messages are displayed in case of exceptions, assisting users in diagnosing and resolving potential issues during operation.
9. Multi-instance Support: The application allows for the simultaneous operation of multiple instances, enabling users to analyze different videos concurrently or compare motion characteristics across multiple instances of the application.
10. Title and Information Display: The GUI dynamically updates the window title to reflect the current state, including the name of the loaded video file. This feature enhances user awareness and provides context within the application interface.

In summary, the project aims to empower users with a versatile tool for motion analysis in videos, combining the computational capabilities of the GBBM algorithm with an intuitive and feature-rich GUI for seamless interaction and analysis.

IMPORTING LIBRARIES

```
import tkinter as tk
from tkinter import ttk
from tkinter import filedialog
from PIL import Image, ImageTk
import imageio
import cv2
import numpy as np
```

This code segment imports necessary libraries for developing a graphical user interface (GUI) application for motion analysis in videos. Here's a brief overview of each imported library:

- tkinter (import tkinter as tk): Tkinter is a standard Python library for creating GUI applications. It provides a set of tools for building windows, buttons, menus, and other GUI elements.
- ttk (from tkinter import ttk): The ttk module in Tkinter provides themed widget classes that offer more modern and visually appealing interfaces compared to the standard Tkinter widgets.
- filedialog (from tkinter import filedialog): The filedialog module provides dialogs for opening and saving files. It allows users to interactively select files or directories from the filesystem.
- PIL (from PIL import Image, ImageTk): PIL (Python Imaging Library) is a library for opening, manipulating, and saving many different image file formats. The Image module provides a class with methods to open, manipulate, and save images, while the ImageTk module provides support for displaying images in Tkinter GUI applications.
- imageio (import imageio): Imageio is a Python library that provides an easy interface to read and write a wide range of image and video file formats. It simplifies the process of working with multimedia data in Python.
- cv2 (import cv2): OpenCV (Open Source Computer Vision Library) is a popular library for computer vision tasks such as image and video processing, object detection, and optical flow estimation. The cv2 module provides Python bindings for OpenCV functions and classes.
- numpy (import numpy as np): NumPy is a fundamental package for scientific computing with Python. It provides support for large, multi-dimensional arrays and matrices, along with a collection of mathematical functions to operate on these arrays efficiently.

By importing these libraries, the code sets the foundation for developing a GUI application with functionalities for loading video files, performing motion analysis using computer vision techniques, and displaying results interactively to the user.

CLASS AND INITIALIZATION

```python
class VideoGBBMOpticalFlow:
    def __init__(self, master):
        self.master = master
        self.master.title("Motion Estimation with Gradient-Based Block Matching Algorithm (GBBM)")
        self.file_name = ""
        self.set_window_title()  # Set window title initially

        # Frame number label
        self.frame_number_label = tk.Label(master, text="Frame: 0")
        self.frame_number_label.pack()

        self.video = None
        self.video_path = None
        self.paused = False
        self.zoom_scale = tk.IntVar(value=1)
        self.frame_index = 0
        self.start_x1 = None
        self.start_y1 = None
        self.current_x1 = 0
        self.current_y1 = 0
        self.start_x2 = None
        self.start_y2 = None
        self.current_x2 = 0
        self.current_y2 = 0

        self.prev_frame_gray = None  # Initialize prev_frame_gray variable
        self.create_widgets()
```

This code defines a class named VideoGBBMOpticalFlow which serves as the backbone for the graphical user interface (GUI) application designed to perform motion estimation using the Gradient-Based Block Matching Algorithm (GBBM) on video data. Let's dissect the initialization method and its attributes:
1. __init__(self, master) Method:
    - This method serves as the constructor for the class, initializing its attributes and setting up the GUI components.

- master: Represents the parent widget (typically a Tkinter Tk instance) to which this GUI component belongs.
2. Attributes:
    - self.master: Stores the reference to the parent widget.
    - self.file_name: Represents the name of the currently loaded video file. Initialized as an empty string.
    - self.frame_number_label: Tkinter Label widget to display the current frame number.
    - self.video: Represents the video object.
    - self.video_path: Stores the path to the currently loaded video file.
    - self.paused: Indicates whether the video playback is paused. Initialized as False.
    - self.zoom_scale: Tkinter IntVar to store the zoom scale value. Initialized with a default value of 1.
    - self.frame_index: Represents the index of the current frame being displayed.
    - self.start_x1, self.start_y1: Stores the initial coordinates of the mouse pointer for canvas 1.
    - self.current_x1, self.current_y1: Stores the current coordinates of the mouse pointer for canvas 1.
    - self.start_x2, self.start_y2: Stores the initial coordinates of the mouse pointer for canvas 2.
    - self.current_x2, self.current_y2: Stores the current coordinates of the mouse pointer for canvas 2.
    - self.prev_frame_gray: Represents the grayscale version of the previous frame. Initialized as None.
3. set_window_title() Method:
    - Updates the window title based on the loaded video file's name.
4. create_widgets() Method:
    - Initializes and configures the GUI components (such as buttons, labels, and canvases) required for video playback and motion analysis.

Overall, this class provides the groundwork for building a user-friendly interface for video motion analysis, with functionalities for loading videos, displaying frames, and potentially visualizing motion estimation results using the GBBM algorithm.

CREATING WIDGETS

```python
    def create_widgets(self):
        # Panel for video display
        video_panel = tk.Frame(self.master)
        video_panel.pack(padx=10, pady=10)

        # Canvas to display the original video
        canvas_width = 800
        canvas_height = 500
        self.canvas = tk.Canvas(video_panel, width=canvas_width, height=canvas_height)
        self.canvas.pack(side="left", fill="both", expand=True)
        self.canvas.bind("<MouseWheel>", self.on_mousewheel)
        self.canvas.bind("<ButtonPress-1>", self.on_press1)
        self.canvas.bind("<B1-Motion>", self.on_drag1)

        # Canvas to display the optical flow result
        self.flow_canvas = tk.Canvas(video_panel, width=canvas_width, height=canvas_height)
        self.flow_canvas.pack(side="right", fill="both", expand=True)
        self.flow_canvas.bind("<MouseWheel>", self.on_mousewheel)
        self.flow_canvas.bind("<ButtonPress-1>", self.on_press2)
        self.flow_canvas.bind("<B1-Motion>", self.on_drag2)

        # Panel for control buttons
        control_panel = tk.Frame(self.master)
        control_panel.pack(padx=10, pady=(0, 10), fill="x")

        # Button to open a video file
        self.open_button = tk.Button(control_panel, text="Open Video", command=self.open_video)
        self.open_button.grid(row=0, column=0, padx=10, pady=5)

        # Combobox for selecting zoom scale
        self.zoom_combobox = ttk.Combobox(control_panel, textvariable=self.zoom_scale, values=list(range(1, 11)))
        self.zoom_combobox.grid(row=0, column=1, padx=10, pady=5)
        self.zoom_combobox.bind("<<ComboboxSelected>>", self.update_zoom)

        # Label and entry for specifying step
        self.step_label = tk.Label(control_panel, text="Step:")
        self.step_label.grid(row=0, column=2, padx=10, pady=5, sticky="e")
        self.step_default = tk.StringVar(value="20")
        self.step_entry = ttk.Entry(control_panel, textvariable=self.step_default)
        self.step_entry.grid(row=0, column=3, padx=10, pady=5, sticky="w")
        self.step_entry.bind("<Return>", lambda event: self.toggle_play_pause())
```

```python
        # Label and entry for specifying dx (same as dy)
        self.dx_label = tk.Label(control_panel, text="dx (same as dy):")
        self.dx_label.grid(row=0, column=4, padx=10, pady=5, sticky="e")
        self.dx_default = tk.StringVar(value="10")
        self.dx_entry = ttk.Entry(control_panel, textvariable=self.dx_default)
        self.dx_entry.grid(row=0, column=5, padx=10, pady=5, sticky="w")
        self.dx_entry.bind("<Return>", lambda event: self.toggle_play_pause())

        # Label and entry for specifying block size
        self.block_size_label = tk.Label(control_panel, text="Block Size:")
        self.block_size_label.grid(row=0, column=6, padx=10, pady=5, sticky="e")
        self.block_size_default = tk.StringVar(value="16")
        self.block_size_entry = ttk.Entry(control_panel,
textvariable=self.block_size_default)
        self.block_size_entry.grid(row=0, column=7, padx=10, pady=5, sticky="w")
        self.block_size_entry.bind("<Return>", lambda event:
self.toggle_play_pause())

        # Label and entry for specifying search range
        self.search_range_label = tk.Label(control_panel, text="Search Range:")
        self.search_range_label.grid(row=0, column=8, padx=10, pady=5, sticky="e")
        self.search_range_default = tk.StringVar(value="16")
        self.search_range_entry = ttk.Entry(control_panel,
textvariable=self.search_range_default)
        self.search_range_entry.grid(row=0, column=9, padx=10, pady=5, sticky="w")
        self.search_range_entry.bind("<Return>", lambda event:
self.toggle_play_pause())

        # Button to jump to specified time
        self.jump_button = tk.Button(control_panel, text="Jump to Time",
command=self.jump_to_time)
        self.jump_button.grid(row=0, column=10, padx=10, pady=5)

        # Button to play/pause the video
        self.play_button = tk.Button(control_panel, text="Play/Pause",
command=self.toggle_play_pause)
        self.play_button.grid(row=0, column=11, padx=10, pady=5)

        # Button to stop the video
        self.stop_button = tk.Button(control_panel, text="Stop",
command=self.stop_video)
        self.stop_button.grid(row=0, column=12, padx=10, pady=5)

        # Button to navigate to the previous frame
        self.prev_frame_button = tk.Button(control_panel, text="Previous Frame",
command=self.prev_frame)
        self.prev_frame_button.grid(row=2, column=1, padx=10, pady=5)
```

```
    # Button to navigate to the next frame
    self.next_frame_button = tk.Button(control_panel, text="Next Frame", command=self.next_frame)
    self.next_frame_button.grid(row=2, column=2, padx=10, pady=5)

    # Button to open another instance of the application
    self.open_another_button = tk.Button(control_panel, text="Open Another Video Player", command=self.open_another_player)
    self.open_another_button.grid(row=2, column=0, columnspan=15, padx=10, pady=5)
```

The create_widgets() method initializes and configures various GUI components for the video display, control buttons, and parameter inputs. Here's a breakdown of each component:

1. Video Display:

    Two canvases are created within a frame (video_panel):
    - self.canvas: Canvas to display the original video frames.
    - self.flow_canvas: Canvas to display the optical flow results.

2. Control Buttons:

    These buttons are placed within a separate frame (control_panel) for better organization.
    - "Open Video": Opens a file dialog to select a video file for analysis.
    - "Jump to Time": Jumps to a specified time in the video.
    - "Play/Pause": Toggles between playing and pausing the video.
    - "Stop": Stops the video playback.
    - "Previous Frame": Navigates to the previous frame.
    - "Next Frame": Navigates to the next frame.
    - "Open Another Video Player": Opens another instance of the application for simultaneous analysis or comparison.

3. Parameter Inputs:

    Entry fields and labels are provided for specifying various parameters related to motion analysis:
    - "Step": Specifies the step size for motion analysis.
    - "dx (same as dy)": Specifies the displacement for motion analysis in both x and y directions.
    - "Block Size": Specifies the size of the blocks used in the block matching algorithm.

- "Search Range": Specifies the search range for motion estimation.
4. Zoom Scale Selection:

    A combobox (self.zoom_combobox) allows users to select the zoom scale for video display, ranging from 1 to 10.
5. Event Bindings:

    Event bindings are set up for mouse wheel scrolling (<MouseWheel>) and mouse interactions (<ButtonPress-1>, <B1-Motion>) to enable functionalities such as zooming and dragging.

Overall, this method sets up the user interface with all the necessary components and functionalities required for video playback, motion analysis, and parameter adjustment.

CONTROLLING VIDEO PLAYBACK

```python
def open_video(self):
    self.video_path = filedialog.askopenfilename(filetypes=[("Video files", "*.mp4;*.avi;*.mkv")])
    if self.video_path:
        self.video = imageio.get_reader(self.video_path)
        self.file_name = self.video_path.split('/')[-1]  # Extract file name
        self.set_window_title()  # Update window title with file name
        self.play_video()

def play_video(self):
    if self.video:
        self.paused = False
        self.show_frame()
        self.show_optical_flow()

def stop_video(self):
    self.paused = True
    self.frame_index = 0
    self.current_x1 = 0
    self.current_y1 = 0  # Reset the current position
    self.show_frame()
    self.show_optical_flow()

def toggle_play_pause(self):
    self.paused = not self.paused
    if not self.paused:
        self.play_video()
```

These methods handle the functionality related to opening, playing, pausing, and stopping the video playback. Here's a breakdown of each method:

1. open_video(self) Method:
   - Opens a file dialog (filedialog.askopenfilename) to select a video file for analysis.
   - If a video file is selected (if self.video_path), it uses imageio.get_reader to create a video reader object.
   - Extracts the file name from the full path and updates self.file_name.
   - Updates the window title with the selected file name using self.set_window_title().
   - Calls self.play_video() to start video playback.

2. play_video(self) Method:
   - Initiates the playback of the video.
   - Sets self.paused to False to indicate that the video is playing.
   - Calls self.show_frame() and self.show_optical_flow() to display the current frame and optical flow.

3. stop_video(self) Method:
   - Stops the video playback.
   - Sets self.paused to True to pause the video.
   - Resets self.frame_index to 0 to go back to the first frame.
   - Resets the current position (self.current_x1 and self.current_y1).
   - Calls self.show_frame() and self.show_optical_flow() to update the display.

4. toggle_play_pause(self) Method:
   - Toggles between playing and pausing the video.
   - Inverts the value of self.paused.
   - If the video is not paused (if not self.paused), it calls self.play_video() to start or resume video playback.

These methods collectively provide control over the video playback, allowing the user to open, play, pause, and stop the video as needed during analysis.

SHOWING FRAME

```
def show_frame(self):
```

```python
        if self.video:
            if not self.paused:
                if 0 <= self.frame_index < len(self.video):  # Check if frame index is within range
                    try:
                        frame = self.video.get_data(self.frame_index)
                        frame_gray = cv2.cvtColor(frame, cv2.COLOR_RGB2GRAY)  # Convert to grayscale

                        # Initialize prev_frame_gray on first frame
                        if self.prev_frame_gray is None:
                            self.prev_frame_gray = frame_gray.copy()

                        # Display current frame
                        frame = Image.fromarray(frame)
                        frame = frame.resize((frame.width * self.zoom_scale.get(), frame.height * self.zoom_scale.get()))
                        photo = ImageTk.PhotoImage(frame)
                        self.photo = photo  # Save object reference to PhotoImage globally
                        self.canvas.delete("video")  # Delete previous image
                        self.canvas.create_image(self.current_x1, self.current_y1, anchor="nw", image=photo, tags="video")

                        # Update prev_frame_gray
                        self.prev_frame_gray = frame_gray.copy()

                        # Update frame number label
                        self.frame_number_label.config(text=f"Frame: {self.frame_index} / {self.video.count_frames()}", font=("Helvetica", 18))

                        self.frame_index += 1  # Move to the next frame

                    except Exception as e:
                        print("Error: ", e)
```

This show_frame() method is responsible for displaying the current frame of the video. Let's break down its functionality:
1. Condition Checks:
    - It first checks if a video is loaded (if self.video) and if the playback is not paused (if not self.paused).
    - Then, it ensures that the frame_index is within the valid range of frames in the video (if 0 <= self.frame_index < len(self.video)).
2. Frame Retrieval and Processing:

- If the conditions are met, it retrieves the current frame using self.video.get_data(self.frame_index).
- Converts the frame to grayscale using OpenCV's cv2.cvtColor() function.
- Initializes prev_frame_gray with the first grayscale frame if it's not already initialized.
3. Displaying the Frame:
    - Converts the frame to a PIL Image object.
    - Resizes the image based on the zoom scale selected by the user.
    - Converts the resized image to a PhotoImage object.
    - Deletes the previous image from the canvas (self.canvas.delete("video")).
    - Creates a new image on the canvas with the current frame, applying any positional adjustments made by the user.
4. Updating UI Elements:
   Updates the frame number label to display the current frame index and the total number of frames in the video.
5. Incrementing Frame Index:
   Increments the frame_index to move to the next frame for subsequent calls to show_frame.
6. Error Handling:
   Catches and prints any exceptions that may occur during the process.

This method ensures smooth and sequential display of frames while updating UI elements to provide users with information about the current frame being displayed.

IMPLEMENTING GRADIENT BASED BLOCK MATCHING

```python
def gradient_based_block_matching(self, prev_frame_gray, frame_gray):
    # GBBM implementation
    block_size = int(self.block_size_entry.get())  # Get block size from entry
    search_range = int(self.search_range_entry.get())  # Get search range from entry
    motion_vectors = np.zeros((frame_gray.shape[0] // block_size, frame_gray.shape[1] // block_size, 2))

    # Compute gradient of the previous frame
    grad_x_prev = cv2.Sobel(prev_frame_gray, cv2.CV_64F, 1, 0, ksize=3)
    grad_y_prev = cv2.Sobel(prev_frame_gray, cv2.CV_64F, 0, 1, ksize=3)
```

```python
        for y in range(0, frame_gray.shape[0] - block_size, block_size):
            for x in range(0, frame_gray.shape[1] - block_size, block_size):
                min_cost = float('inf')
                best_dx = 0
                best_dy = 0
                for dy in range(-search_range, search_range + 1):
                    for dx in range(-search_range, search_range + 1):
                        # Ensure the search area is within frame boundaries
                        if 0 <= y + dy < frame_gray.shape[0] - block_size and 0 <= x + dx < frame_gray.shape[1] - block_size:
                            template = prev_frame_gray[y:y+block_size, x:x+block_size]
                            search_area = frame_gray[y+dy:y+dy+block_size, x+dx:x+dx+block_size]

                            # Compute gradient of the search area
                            grad_x_search = cv2.Sobel(search_area, cv2.CV_64F, 1, 0, ksize=3)
                            grad_y_search = cv2.Sobel(search_area, cv2.CV_64F, 0, 1, ksize=3)

                            # Compute sum of squared differences of gradients
                            ssd_grad = np.sum((grad_x_prev[y:y+block_size, x:x+block_size] - grad_x_search)**2 + (grad_y_prev[y:y+block_size, x:x+block_size] - grad_y_search)**2)
                            if ssd_grad < min_cost:
                                min_cost = ssd_grad
                                best_dx = dx
                                best_dy = dy
                motion_vectors[y // block_size, x // block_size] = [best_dx, best_dy]

        return motion_vectors
```

Let's delve into the workings of the Gradient-Based Block Matching Algorithm (GBBM) implemented in the gradient_based_block_matching() method:

1. Objective:
   The primary goal of this algorithm is to estimate the motion between consecutive frames in a video sequence. It does so by comparing blocks of pixels between frames and determining the best match, often referred to as a motion vector, which represents the displacement of a block from one frame to another.
2. Parameters:
   - prev_frame_gray: This parameter represents the grayscale version of the previous frame, essential for computing the gradients and comparing blocks.

- frame_gray: Similarly, this parameter is the grayscale version of the current frame, which is used to find matching blocks.
3. Block Matching:
    - The algorithm operates by dividing the current frame into blocks of pixels, each typically of a fixed size specified by the user. For each block in the current frame, it searches for a matching block in the previous frame.
    - This search is performed within a defined search range around the block's position in the current frame. The search range determines how far the algorithm will look for a match.
4. Gradient Calculation:
    - Before comparing blocks, the gradients of the previous frame are calculated using Sobel filters in both the x and y directions. These gradients provide information about the spatial changes in intensity, which are crucial for motion estimation.
5. Block Comparison:
    - For each block in the current frame, the algorithm iterates through possible displacements within the search range and computes a similarity metric between the block and all candidate blocks in the previous frame.
    - The similarity metric is based on the sum of squared differences (SSD) of gradients between the corresponding regions in the previous and current frames. This metric indicates how closely two blocks resemble each other.
6. Motion Vector Determination:
    - The algorithm selects the displacement (motion vector) that minimizes the SSD metric. This displacement represents the motion between the current block and its best-matching block in the previous frame.
    - Once the best match is found, the corresponding motion vector (dx, dy) is assigned to the block.
7. Output:
    - The output of the algorithm is an array of motion vectors, where each vector corresponds to a block in the current frame. These vectors collectively represent the motion across the entire frame.
    - These motion vectors can be further utilized for tasks such as optical flow visualization, object tracking, or video compression.
8. Complexity:

The computational complexity of this algorithm depends on factors such as the block size, search range, and frame resolution. Larger block sizes and search ranges lead to increased computation time but may yield more accurate motion estimation.

In summary, the Gradient-Based Block Matching Algorithm is a fundamental technique for motion estimation in video processing, leveraging gradients and block comparison to accurately determine motion vectors between consecutive frames.

The Gradient-Based Block Matching Algorithm (GBBM) is a technique used in motion estimation, a fundamental process in video processing and computer vision. It's primarily utilized in tasks like video compression, object tracking, and motion analysis. Here's a detailed explanation of how the GBBM algorithm works:

1. Motion Estimation:
   The primary objective of motion estimation is to compute the motion between consecutive frames in a video sequence. This motion is often represented as motion vectors, which describe the displacement of blocks or regions between frames.
2. Block Matching:
   GBBM operates on the principle of block matching, where each frame is divided into smaller blocks of pixels. For each block in the current frame, the algorithm searches for the most similar block in the previous frame.
3. Gradients:
   Before comparing blocks, gradients are computed for both frames. Gradients provide information about the rate of change of pixel intensities in different directions (typically horizontal and vertical).
4. Block Comparison:
   - For each block in the current frame, the algorithm searches for a matching block in the previous frame. It does so by comparing the intensity values (or features) of pixels within the blocks.
   - A common metric used for comparison is the sum of squared differences (SSD) or other similarity measures. SSD calculates the difference between corresponding pixels in the two blocks and sums up these differences.
5. Search Strategy:
   - The search for matching blocks is performed within a specified search range around each block's position in the current frame. This range determines how far the algorithm will look for a match.
   - GBBM typically employs exhaustive search, where all possible displacements within the search range are considered. Other search

strategies like hierarchical search or predictive search can also be used to improve efficiency.
6. Motion Vector Determination:
   - The displacement (motion vector) that minimizes the similarity metric (e.g., SSD) is selected as the best match. This displacement represents the motion between the current block and its best-matching block in the previous frame.
   - The motion vector (dx, dy) indicates the horizontal and vertical displacement of the block.
7. Motion Field:
After computing motion vectors for all blocks in the frame, the result is a motion field that describes the motion of different regions in the frame. This motion field can be visualized or used for subsequent video processing tasks.
8. Parameters:
GBBM's performance and accuracy can be influenced by parameters such as block size (size of the blocks used for comparison), search range (maximum displacement considered), and similarity metric used for comparison.
9. Applications:
GBBM finds applications in various fields, including video compression (motion compensation in predictive coding), video stabilization, object tracking, and activity recognition.

In summary, the Gradient-Based Block Matching Algorithm is a versatile technique for motion estimation, leveraging block matching and gradient information to accurately determine motion vectors between consecutive frames in a video sequence.

SHOWING OPTICAL FLOW

```
def show_optical_flow(self):
    if self.video:
        if not self.paused:
            if 0 <= self.frame_index < len(self.video):  # Check if frame index is within range
                try:
                    frame = self.video.get_data(self.frame_index)
                    frame_gray = cv2.cvtColor(frame, cv2.COLOR_RGB2GRAY)  # Convert to grayscale
```

```python
                # Calculate optical flow using Gradient-Based Block Matching Algorithm (GBBM)
                motion_vectors = self.gradient_based_block_matching(self.prev_frame_gray, frame_gray)

                # Create an empty mask image for visualization
                mask = np.zeros_like(frame)

                # Compute flow visualization
                step = int(self.step_entry.get())
                for y in range(0, frame.shape[0], step):
                    for x in range(0, frame.shape[1], step):
                        # Ensure the motion vectors index does not exceed the bounds
                        if y // step < motion_vectors.shape[0] and x // step < motion_vectors.shape[1]:
                            dx, dy = motion_vectors[y // step, x // step]
                            # Scale the optical flow vectors based on the zoom scale
                            dx *= int(self.dx_entry.get())
                            dy *= int(self.dx_entry.get())
                            # Convert coordinates to integers
                            x1, y1 = int(x), int(y)
                            x2, y2 = int(x + dx), int(y + dy)
                            # Draw the line and circle
                            cv2.line(mask, (x1, y1), (x2, y2), (255, 255, 255), 1)
                            cv2.circle(mask, (x2, y2), 1, (0, 255, 0), -1)

                # Convert mask to PIL format and display on canvas
                mask = Image.fromarray(mask)
                mask = ImageTk.PhotoImage(mask)
                self.mask = mask
                self.flow_canvas.delete("mask")  # Delete previous optical flow
                self.flow_canvas.create_image(self.current_x2, self.current_y2, anchor="nw", image=mask, tags="mask")

                #self.frame_index += 1  # Move to the next frame

                # Update previous frame
                self.prev_frame_gray = frame_gray.copy()

        except Exception as e:
            print("Error in show_optical_flow:", e)  # Print error message
```

The show_optical_flow() method in your code is responsible for visualizing the optical flow between consecutive frames using the Gradient-Based Block Matching Algorithm (GBBM). Let's break down how it works:
1. Frame Acquisition:
    - It retrieves the current frame from the video using self.video.get_data(self.frame_index).
    - Then, it converts the frame to grayscale using cv2.cvtColor(frame, cv2.COLOR_RGB2GRAY).
2. Optical Flow Calculation:
    The optical flow is computed between the current frame and the previous frame (stored in self.prev_frame_gray) using the gradient_based_block_matching method. This method returns motion vectors representing the displacement of blocks between the frames.
3. Visualization:
    - An empty mask image is created for visualization using np.zeros_like(frame). This mask will be used to draw the optical flow vectors.
    - The algorithm then iterates over the image, drawing a line and a circle for each motion vector.
    - For each block in the frame, it retrieves the corresponding motion vector from the motion_vectors array.
    - The magnitude and direction of the motion vector determine the length and direction of the line drawn from the block's center.
    - The line indicates the direction of motion, and the circle represents the end point of the motion vector.
    - These lines and circles are drawn on the mask image using OpenCV functions like cv2.line and cv2.circle.
4. Display:
    - The mask image, containing the visualized optical flow, is converted to PIL format using Image.fromarray(mask).
    - Then, it's converted to a PhotoImage object using ImageTk.PhotoImage(mask), which can be displayed on the canvas.
    - The previous optical flow visualization is removed from the canvas using self.flow_canvas.delete("mask").
    - Finally, the new optical flow visualization is displayed on the canvas using self.flow_canvas.create_image.

5. Update:

    The prev_frame_gray variable is updated with the current frame, preparing it for the next iteration.

Overall, this method visualizes the optical flow between frames, providing a visual representation of motion in the video sequence.

HANDLING MOUSE EVENTS

```python
def on_mousewheel(self, event):
    direction = event.delta // 120
    current_value = int(self.zoom_scale.get())
    if direction == 1 and current_value < 10:
        current_value += 1
    elif direction == -1 and current_value > 1:
        current_value -= 1
    self.zoom_scale.set(current_value)
    self.update_zoom()

def on_press1(self, event):
    self.start_x1 = event.x
    self.start_y1 = event.y

def on_drag1(self, event):
    if self.start_x1 and self.start_y1:
        self.x_offset1 = event.x - self.start_x1
        self.y_offset1 = event.y - self.start_y1
        self.current_x1 += self.x_offset1  # Update current position
        self.current_y1 += self.y_offset1  # Update current position
        self.canvas.move("video", self.x_offset1, self.y_offset1)
        self.start_x1 = event.x
        self.start_y1 = event.y

def on_press2(self, event):
    self.start_x2 = event.x
    self.start_y2 = event.y

def on_drag2(self, event):
    if self.start_x2 and self.start_y2:
        self.x_offset2 = event.x - self.start_x2
        self.y_offset2 = event.y - self.start_y2
        self.current_x2 += self.x_offset2  # Update current position
        self.current_y2 += self.y_offset2  # Update current position
```

```
        self.flow_canvas.move("mask", self.x_offset2, self.y_offset2)  # Move
optical flow canvas along with original canvas
        self.start_x2 = event.x
        self.start_y2 = event.y
```

These methods handle mouse wheel scrolling and mouse dragging events for the canvas widgets displaying the original video and optical flow visualizations.
1. on_mousewheel() Method:
    - This method is triggered when the user scrolls the mouse wheel.
    - It calculates the direction of scrolling (direction) and the current zoom scale value.
    - If the scrolling direction is upwards (direction == 1) and the current zoom scale is less than 10, it increases the zoom scale value by 1.
    - If the scrolling direction is downwards (direction == -1) and the current zoom scale is greater than 1, it decreases the zoom scale value by 1.
    - Then, it updates the zoom scale value and calls the update_zoom method to apply the new zoom level.
2. on_press1() and on_press2() Methods:
    - These methods are triggered when the user presses the left mouse button (Button-1) on the canvas displaying the original video (on_press1) or the optical flow visualization (on_press2).
    - They store the coordinates of the mouse pointer (event.x and event.y) as the starting position for dragging.
3. on_drag1() and on_drag2() Methods:
    - These methods are triggered when the user drags the mouse while holding down the left mouse button after pressing (Button-1) on the canvas displaying the original video (on_drag1) or the optical flow visualization (on_drag2).
    - They calculate the horizontal and vertical offsets (x_offset and y_offset) by subtracting the current mouse coordinates from the starting coordinates.
    - Then, they update the current position (self.current_x and self.current_y) by adding these offsets.
    - Finally, they move the canvas items ("video" or "mask") by the calculated offsets using the canvas.move or flow_canvas.move methods, respectively.

These methods provide interactivity by allowing the user to zoom in/out and drag the video or optical flow visualization within their respective canvas areas.

NAVIGATING FRAME

```
def prev_frame(self):
    if self.frame_index > 0:
        self.frame_index -= 1
        self.show_frame()
        self.show_optical_flow()
        print(self.frame_index)

def next_frame(self):
    if self.video and self.frame_index < len(self.video) - 1:
        self.show_frame()
        self.show_optical_flow()
        print(self.frame_index)
```

These methods, prev_frame() and next_frame(), are responsible for navigating to the previous and next frames of the video, respectively.

1. prev_frame() Method:
   - It checks if the current frame index is greater than 0, indicating that there are previous frames available.
   - If so, it decrements the frame_index variable by 1 to move to the previous frame.
   - Then, it calls the show_frame() and show_optical_flow() methods to display the previous frame and its optical flow visualization, respectively.
   - Finally, it prints the current frame index to the console.
2. next_frame() Method:
   - It first checks if a video is loaded (self.video) and if the current frame index is less than the total number of frames in the video minus 1.
   - If both conditions are met, it means there are more frames available.
   - Then, it calls the show_frame() and show_optical_flow() methods to display the next frame and its optical flow visualization, respectively.
   - Finally, it prints the current frame index to the console.

These methods provide functionality for stepping through the frames of the video one at a time, allowing users to inspect individual frames and their corresponding optical flow visualizations.

SETTING WINDOW TITLE

```
def set_window_title(self):
    if self.file_name:
        self.master.title(f"Motion Estimation with Gradient-Based Block Matching Algorithm (GBBM) - {self.file_name}")
        self.master.title_font = ("Helvetica", 16, "bold")
    else:
        self.master.title("Motion Estimation with Gradient-Based Block Matching Algorithm (GBBM)")
```

The set_window_title() method is responsible for setting the title of the application window. Here's how it works:
1. Conditions:
   It first checks if self.file_name is not empty, ensuring that a video file has been selected and its name is available.
2. Setting the Title:
   - If a file name is available, it constructs a title string that includes the name of the selected video file. It uses an f-string to insert the file name into a predefined title format.
   - The title format includes a descriptive prefix ("Motion Estimation with Gradient-Based Block Matching Algorithm (GBBM) - "), followed by the actual file name.
3. Formatting:
   It also sets the title font to be bold and larger for better visibility.

This method ensures that the application window title reflects the selected video file's name, providing users with context about the video being analyzed for motion estimation using the Gradient-Based Block Matching Algorithm. If no file is selected, it sets a default title without the file name.

RUNNING PROGRAM

Run program and click on Open Video button. Then, choose a video file then click on Next Frame button.

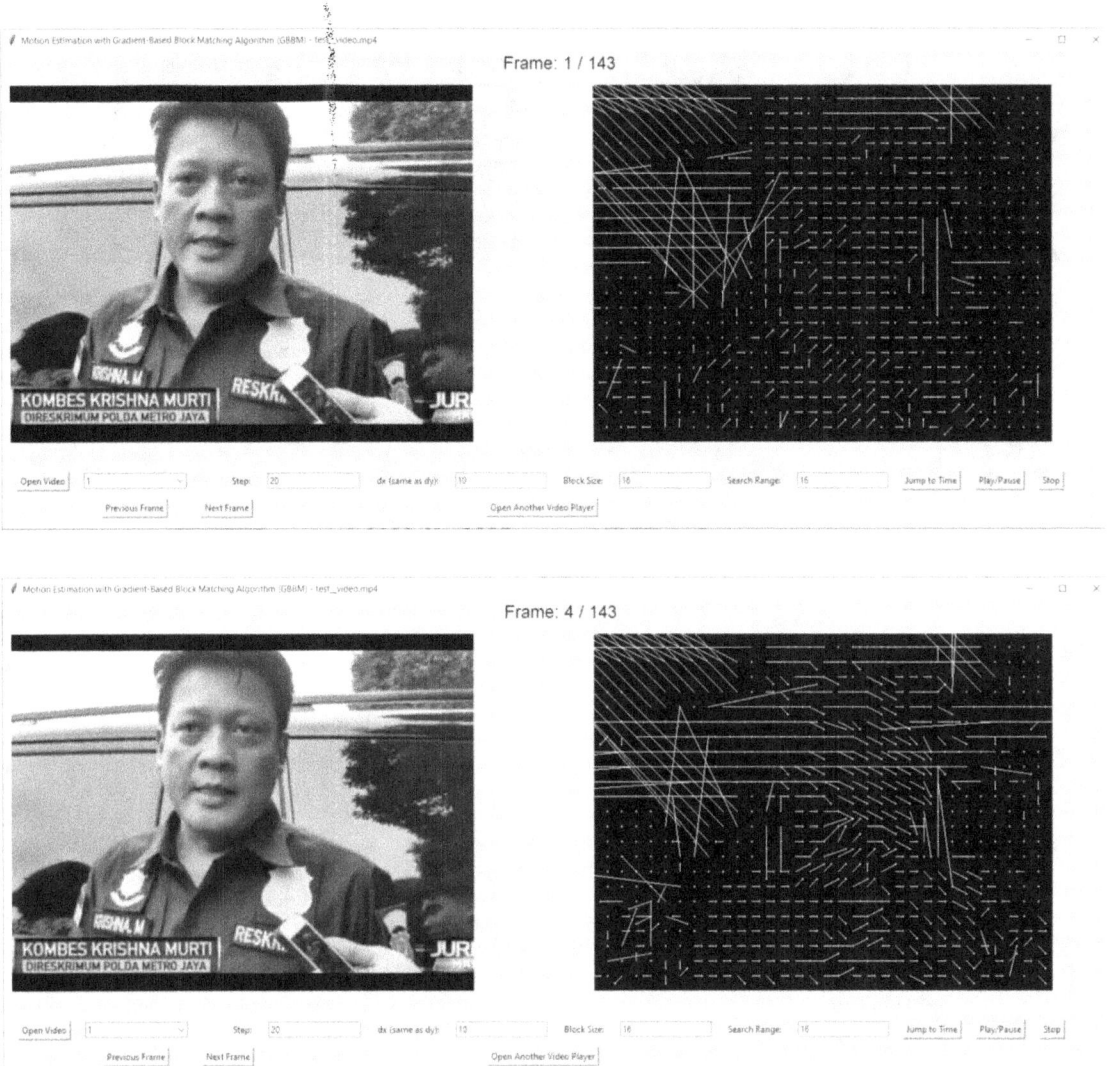

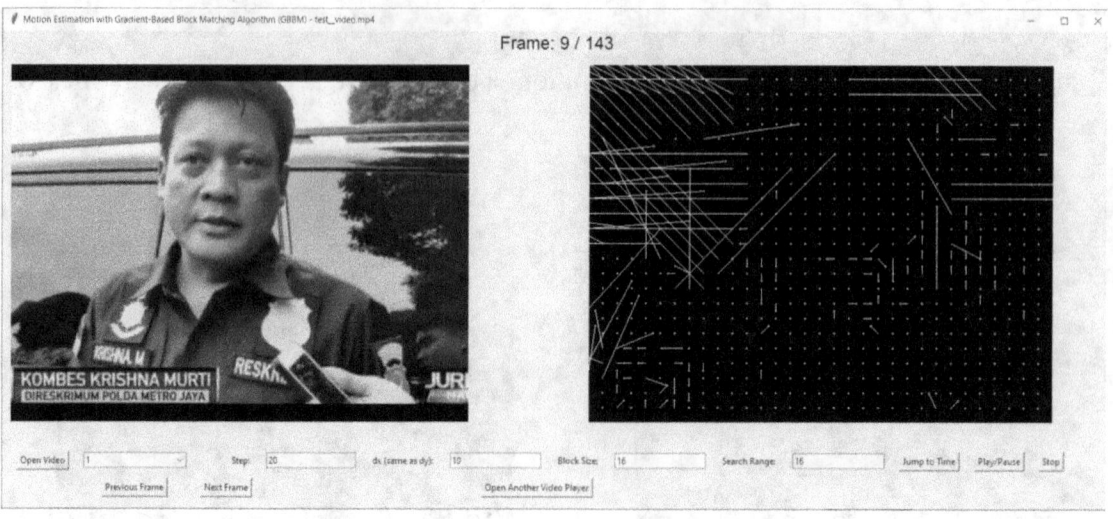

SOURCE CODE

```
#gui_motion_analysis_gbbm.py
import tkinter as tk
from tkinter import ttk
from tkinter import filedialog
from PIL import Image, ImageTk
import imageio
import cv2
import numpy as np

class VideoGBBMOpticalFlow:
    def __init__(self, master):
        self.master = master
        self.master.title("Motion Estimation with Gradient-Based Block Matching Algorithm (GBBM)")
        self.file_name = ""
        self.set_window_title()  # Set window title initially

        # Frame number label
        self.frame_number_label = tk.Label(master, text="Frame: 0")
        self.frame_number_label.pack()

        self.video = None
        self.video_path = None
        self.paused = False
        self.zoom_scale = tk.IntVar(value=1)
        self.frame_index = 0
        self.start_x1 = None
```

```python
        self.start_y1 = None
        self.current_x1 = 0
        self.current_y1 = 0
        self.start_x2 = None
        self.start_y2 = None
        self.current_x2 = 0
        self.current_y2 = 0

        self.prev_frame_gray = None  # Initialize prev_frame_gray variable
        self.create_widgets()

    def create_widgets(self):
        # Panel for video display
        video_panel = tk.Frame(self.master)
        video_panel.pack(padx=10, pady=10)

        # Canvas to display the original video
        canvas_width = 800
        canvas_height = 500
        self.canvas = tk.Canvas(video_panel, width=canvas_width, height=canvas_height)
        self.canvas.pack(side="left", fill="both", expand=True)
        self.canvas.bind("<MouseWheel>", self.on_mousewheel)
        self.canvas.bind("<ButtonPress-1>", self.on_press1)
        self.canvas.bind("<B1-Motion>", self.on_drag1)

        # Canvas to display the optical flow result
        self.flow_canvas = tk.Canvas(video_panel, width=canvas_width, height=canvas_height)
        self.flow_canvas.pack(side="right", fill="both", expand=True)
        self.flow_canvas.bind("<MouseWheel>", self.on_mousewheel)
        self.flow_canvas.bind("<ButtonPress-1>", self.on_press2)
        self.flow_canvas.bind("<B1-Motion>", self.on_drag2)

        # Panel for control buttons
        control_panel = tk.Frame(self.master)
        control_panel.pack(padx=10, pady=(0, 10), fill="x")

        # Button to open a video file
        self.open_button = tk.Button(control_panel, text="Open Video", command=self.open_video)
        self.open_button.grid(row=0, column=0, padx=10, pady=5)

        # Combobox for selecting zoom scale
        self.zoom_combobox = ttk.Combobox(control_panel, textvariable=self.zoom_scale, values=list(range(1, 11)))
        self.zoom_combobox.grid(row=0, column=1, padx=10, pady=5)
        self.zoom_combobox.bind("<<ComboboxSelected>>", self.update_zoom)
```

```python
        # Label and entry for specifying step
        self.step_label = tk.Label(control_panel, text="Step:")
        self.step_label.grid(row=0, column=2, padx=10, pady=5, sticky="e")
        self.step_default = tk.StringVar(value="20")
        self.step_entry = ttk.Entry(control_panel, textvariable=self.step_default)
        self.step_entry.grid(row=0, column=3, padx=10, pady=5, sticky="w")
        self.step_entry.bind("<Return>", lambda event: self.toggle_play_pause())

        # Label and entry for specifying dx (same as dy)
        self.dx_label = tk.Label(control_panel, text="dx (same as dy):")
        self.dx_label.grid(row=0, column=4, padx=10, pady=5, sticky="e")
        self.dx_default = tk.StringVar(value="10")
        self.dx_entry = ttk.Entry(control_panel, textvariable=self.dx_default)
        self.dx_entry.grid(row=0, column=5, padx=10, pady=5, sticky="w")
        self.dx_entry.bind("<Return>", lambda event: self.toggle_play_pause())

        # Label and entry for specifying block size
        self.block_size_label = tk.Label(control_panel, text="Block Size:")
        self.block_size_label.grid(row=0, column=6, padx=10, pady=5, sticky="e")
        self.block_size_default = tk.StringVar(value="16")
        self.block_size_entry = ttk.Entry(control_panel, textvariable=self.block_size_default)
        self.block_size_entry.grid(row=0, column=7, padx=10, pady=5, sticky="w")
        self.block_size_entry.bind("<Return>", lambda event: self.toggle_play_pause())

        # Label and entry for specifying search range
        self.search_range_label = tk.Label(control_panel, text="Search Range:")
        self.search_range_label.grid(row=0, column=8, padx=10, pady=5, sticky="e")
        self.search_range_default = tk.StringVar(value="16")
        self.search_range_entry = ttk.Entry(control_panel, textvariable=self.search_range_default)
        self.search_range_entry.grid(row=0, column=9, padx=10, pady=5, sticky="w")
        self.search_range_entry.bind("<Return>", lambda event: self.toggle_play_pause())

        # Button to jump to specified time
        self.jump_button = tk.Button(control_panel, text="Jump to Time", command=self.jump_to_time)
        self.jump_button.grid(row=0, column=10, padx=10, pady=5)

        # Button to play/pause the video
        self.play_button = tk.Button(control_panel, text="Play/Pause", command=self.toggle_play_pause)
        self.play_button.grid(row=0, column=11, padx=10, pady=5)

        # Button to stop the video
```

```python
        self.stop_button = tk.Button(control_panel, text="Stop", 
command=self.stop_video)
        self.stop_button.grid(row=0, column=12, padx=10, pady=5)

        # Button to navigate to the previous frame
        self.prev_frame_button = tk.Button(control_panel, text="Previous Frame", 
command=self.prev_frame)
        self.prev_frame_button.grid(row=2, column=1, padx=10, pady=5)

        # Button to navigate to the next frame
        self.next_frame_button = tk.Button(control_panel, text="Next Frame", 
command=self.next_frame)
        self.next_frame_button.grid(row=2, column=2, padx=10, pady=5)

        # Button to open another instance of the application
        self.open_another_button = tk.Button(control_panel, text="Open Another Video 
Player", command=self.open_another_player)
        self.open_another_button.grid(row=2, column=0, columnspan=15, padx=10, 
pady=5)

    def open_video(self):
        self.video_path = filedialog.askopenfilename(filetypes=[("Video files", 
"*.mp4;*.avi;*.mkv")])
        if self.video_path:
            self.video = imageio.get_reader(self.video_path)
            self.file_name = self.video_path.split('/')[-1]  # Extract file name
            self.set_window_title()  # Update window title with file name
            self.play_video()

    def play_video(self):
        if self.video:
            self.paused = False
            self.show_frame()
            self.show_optical_flow()

    def stop_video(self):
        self.paused = True
        self.frame_index = 0
        self.current_x1 = 0
        self.current_y1 = 0  # Reset the current position
        self.show_frame()
        self.show_optical_flow()

    def toggle_play_pause(self):
        self.paused = not self.paused
        if not self.paused:
            self.play_video()
```

```python
    def update_zoom(self, event=None):
        self.show_frame()
        self.show_optical_flow()

    def show_frame(self):
        if self.video:
            if not self.paused:
                if 0 <= self.frame_index < len(self.video):  # Check if frame index is within range
                    try:
                        frame = self.video.get_data(self.frame_index)
                        frame_gray = cv2.cvtColor(frame, cv2.COLOR_RGB2GRAY)  # Convert to grayscale

                        # Initialize prev_frame_gray on first frame
                        if self.prev_frame_gray is None:
                            self.prev_frame_gray = frame_gray.copy()

                        # Display current frame
                        frame = Image.fromarray(frame)
                        frame = frame.resize((frame.width * self.zoom_scale.get(), frame.height * self.zoom_scale.get()))
                        photo = ImageTk.PhotoImage(frame)
                        self.photo = photo  # Save object reference to PhotoImage globally
                        self.canvas.delete("video")  # Delete previous image
                        self.canvas.create_image(self.current_x1, self.current_y1, anchor="nw", image=photo, tags="video")

                        # Update prev_frame_gray
                        self.prev_frame_gray = frame_gray.copy()

                        # Update frame number label
                        self.frame_number_label.config(text=f"Frame: {self.frame_index} / {self.video.count_frames()}", font=("Helvetica", 18))

                        self.frame_index += 1  # Move to the next frame

                    except Exception as e:
                        print("Error: ", e)

    def gradient_based_block_matching(self, prev_frame_gray, frame_gray):
        # GBBM implementation
        block_size = int(self.block_size_entry.get())  # Get block size from entry
        search_range = int(self.search_range_entry.get())  # Get search range from entry

        motion_vectors = np.zeros((frame_gray.shape[0] // block_size, frame_gray.shape[1] // block_size, 2))
```

```python
            # Compute gradient of the previous frame
            grad_x_prev = cv2.Sobel(prev_frame_gray, cv2.CV_64F, 1, 0, ksize=3)
            grad_y_prev = cv2.Sobel(prev_frame_gray, cv2.CV_64F, 0, 1, ksize=3)

            for y in range(0, frame_gray.shape[0] - block_size, block_size):
                for x in range(0, frame_gray.shape[1] - block_size, block_size):
                    min_cost = float('inf')
                    best_dx = 0
                    best_dy = 0
                    for dy in range(-search_range, search_range + 1):
                        for dx in range(-search_range, search_range + 1):
                            # Ensure the search area is within frame boundaries
                            if 0 <= y + dy < frame_gray.shape[0] - block_size and 0 <= x + dx < frame_gray.shape[1] - block_size:
                                template = prev_frame_gray[y:y+block_size, x:x+block_size]
                                search_area = frame_gray[y+dy:y+dy+block_size, x+dx:x+dx+block_size]

                                # Compute gradient of the search area
                                grad_x_search = cv2.Sobel(search_area, cv2.CV_64F, 1, 0, ksize=3)
                                grad_y_search = cv2.Sobel(search_area, cv2.CV_64F, 0, 1, ksize=3)

                                # Compute sum of squared differences of gradients
                                ssd_grad = np.sum((grad_x_prev[y:y+block_size, x:x+block_size] - grad_x_search)**2 + (grad_y_prev[y:y+block_size, x:x+block_size] - grad_y_search)**2)
                                if ssd_grad < min_cost:
                                    min_cost = ssd_grad
                                    best_dx = dx
                                    best_dy = dy
                    motion_vectors[y // block_size, x // block_size] = [best_dx, best_dy]

        return motion_vectors

    def show_optical_flow(self):
        if self.video:
            if not self.paused:
                if 0 <= self.frame_index < len(self.video):  # Check if frame index is within range
                    try:
                        frame = self.video.get_data(self.frame_index)
                        frame_gray = cv2.cvtColor(frame, cv2.COLOR_RGB2GRAY)  # Convert to grayscale
```

```python
                        # Calculate optical flow using Gradient-Based Block Matching Algorithm (GBBM)
                        motion_vectors = self.gradient_based_block_matching(self.prev_frame_gray, frame_gray)

                        # Create an empty mask image for visualization
                        mask = np.zeros_like(frame)

                        # Compute flow visualization
                        step = int(self.step_entry.get())
                        for y in range(0, frame.shape[0], step):
                            for x in range(0, frame.shape[1], step):
                                # Ensure the motion vectors index does not exceed the bounds
                                if y // step < motion_vectors.shape[0] and x // step < motion_vectors.shape[1]:
                                    dx, dy = motion_vectors[y // step, x // step]
                                    # Scale the optical flow vectors based on the zoom scale
                                    dx *= int(self.dx_entry.get())
                                    dy *= int(self.dx_entry.get())
                                    # Convert coordinates to integers
                                    x1, y1 = int(x), int(y)
                                    x2, y2 = int(x + dx), int(y + dy)
                                    # Draw the line and circle
                                    cv2.line(mask, (x1, y1), (x2, y2), (255, 255, 255), 1)
                                    cv2.circle(mask, (x2, y2), 1, (0, 255, 0), -1)

                        # Convert mask to PIL format and display on canvas
                        mask = Image.fromarray(mask)
                        mask = ImageTk.PhotoImage(mask)
                        self.mask = mask
                        self.flow_canvas.delete("mask")  # Delete previous optical flow
                        self.flow_canvas.create_image(self.current_x2, self.current_y2, anchor="nw", image=mask, tags="mask")

                        #self.frame_index += 1  # Move to the next frame

                        # Update previous frame
                        self.prev_frame_gray = frame_gray.copy()

                except Exception as e:
                    print("Error in show_optical_flow:", e)  # Print error message

    def on_mousewheel(self, event):
```

```python
            direction = event.delta // 120
            current_value = int(self.zoom_scale.get())
            if direction == 1 and current_value < 10:
                current_value += 1
            elif direction == -1 and current_value > 1:
                current_value -= 1
            self.zoom_scale.set(current_value)
            self.update_zoom()

    def on_press1(self, event):
        self.start_x1 = event.x
        self.start_y1 = event.y

    def on_drag1(self, event):
        if self.start_x1 and self.start_y1:
            self.x_offset1 = event.x - self.start_x1
            self.y_offset1 = event.y - self.start_y1
            self.current_x1 += self.x_offset1  # Update current position
            self.current_y1 += self.y_offset1  # Update current position
            self.canvas.move("video", self.x_offset1, self.y_offset1)
            self.start_x1 = event.x
            self.start_y1 = event.y

    def on_press2(self, event):
        self.start_x2 = event.x
        self.start_y2 = event.y

    def on_drag2(self, event):
        if self.start_x2 and self.start_y2:
            self.x_offset2 = event.x - self.start_x2
            self.y_offset2 = event.y - self.start_y2
            self.current_x2 += self.x_offset2  # Update current position
            self.current_y2 += self.y_offset2  # Update current position
            self.flow_canvas.move("mask", self.x_offset2, self.y_offset2)  # Move
optical flow canvas along with original canvas
            self.start_x2 = event.x
            self.start_y2 = event.y

    def jump_to_time(self):
        time_str = self.time_entry.get()
        try:
            time_seconds = float(time_str)
            if 0 <= time_seconds:
                self.frame_index = int(time_seconds * self.video.get_meta_data()['fps'])
                self.show_frame()
                self.show_optical_flow()  # Jump to specified time for optical flow
        except ValueError:
```

```python
            pass

    def prev_frame(self):
        if self.frame_index > 0:
            self.frame_index -= 1
            self.show_frame()
            self.show_optical_flow()
            print(self.frame_index)

    def next_frame(self):
        if self.video and self.frame_index < len(self.video) - 1:
            self.show_frame()
            self.show_optical_flow()
            print(self.frame_index)

    def set_window_title(self):
        if self.file_name:
            self.master.title(f"Motion Estimation with Gradient-Based Block Matching Algorithm (GBBM) - {self.file_name}")
            self.master.title_font = ("Helvetica", 16, "bold")
        else:
            self.master.title("Motion Estimation with Gradient-Based Block Matching Algorithm (GBBM)")

    def open_another_player(self):
        # Open another instance of the application
        root = tk.Toplevel(self.master)
        app = VideoGBBMOpticalFlow(root)

def main():
    root = tk.Tk()
    app = VideoGBBMOpticalFlow(root)
    root.mainloop()

if __name__ == "__main__":
    main()
```

MOTION ESTIMATION WITH GRADIENT-BASED BLOCK MATCHING ALGORITHM (GBBM) WITH PYRAMID APPROACH

DESCRIPTION

The project gui_motion_analysis_gbbm_pyramid.py aims to provide a user-friendly interface for analyzing motion in videos using the Gradient-Based Block Matching Algorithm (GBBM) with a Pyramid Approach. The purpose of this project can be understood in several aspects.

Firstly, it addresses the need for motion analysis in video processing applications. Motion estimation is a crucial task in various fields such as computer vision, video surveillance, and robotics. By providing a GUI interface, the project makes motion analysis more accessible to users who may not have expertise in programming or computer vision algorithms.

Secondly, the project leverages the GBBM algorithm, a widely used technique for motion estimation in video processing. GBBM works by comparing blocks of pixels between consecutive frames to detect motion. By implementing this algorithm in a GUI application, users can visualize and analyze the detected motion more intuitively, enhancing their understanding of the video content.

Thirdly, the inclusion of a Pyramid Approach in the GBBM algorithm enhances its performance and robustness. The Pyramid Approach involves constructing image pyramids at multiple resolutions, allowing for more accurate motion estimation across different scales. This ensures that the motion estimation algorithm can handle various types of motion, including large-scale and small-scale movements, effectively.

Moreover, the project provides various control options and visualization features to enhance user experience and facilitate detailed analysis. Users can control parameters such as zoom scale, step size, block size, and search range, allowing them to customize the motion analysis process according to their specific requirements. Additionally, the GUI interface displays the original video frames and the computed optical flow results side by side, enabling users to visually inspect the detected motion.

Overall, the project aims to democratize motion analysis in videos by providing a user-friendly interface powered by state-of-the-art algorithms. By combining the GBBM algorithm with a Pyramid Approach and integrating it into a GUI application, the project empowers users to perform detailed motion analysis tasks with ease and efficiency, fostering advancements in various domains that rely on video processing and analysis.

IMPLEMENTING GRADIENT-BASED BLOCK MACHING WITH PYRAMID APPROACH

The Gradient-Based Block Matching (GBBM) algorithm with a Pyramid Approach is a technique used for motion estimation in video processing. It's an extension of the basic block matching algorithm that enhances its performance and robustness by incorporating a multi-resolution pyramid strategy.

Here's a detailed explanation of how the GBBM algorithm with a Pyramid Approach works:

1. Pyramid Construction:
   The first step in the Pyramid Approach is to construct image pyramids at multiple resolutions. This involves creating a series of downsampled versions of the original image, forming a hierarchical structure resembling a pyramid. Each level of the pyramid represents the image at a different scale, with the top level being the original resolution and subsequent levels having reduced resolutions.
2. Motion Estimation at Different Resolutions:
   - The GBBM algorithm is applied independently at each level of the pyramid. Starting from the highest resolution (original image), motion estimation is performed between consecutive frames using block matching.
   - At higher resolutions, the algorithm detects finer details and small-scale motion, while at lower resolutions, it captures larger-scale motion. This multi-resolution approach allows the algorithm to handle a wide range of motion dynamics effectively.
3. Adjustment of Parameters:
   - As the algorithm operates at different resolutions, certain parameters such as block size and search range need to be adjusted accordingly. Typically, these parameters are scaled based on the resolution of the image being processed.
   - For example, at higher resolutions, smaller block sizes and search ranges are used to capture finer details, whereas at lower resolutions, larger block sizes and search ranges are employed to detect larger-scale motion.
4. Integration of Pyramid Levels:
   - After motion estimation is performed at each level of the pyramid, the results are integrated or combined to obtain the final motion vectors. This integration process involves aligning the motion vectors from different levels of the pyramid to ensure consistency across scales.
   - Depending on the application, various integration strategies can be employed, such as weighted averaging or hierarchical refinement.
5. Flow Visualization and Analysis:
   - Finally, the computed motion vectors are used to generate optical flow fields, visualizing the motion patterns within the video sequence. These optical flow fields provide valuable insights into the dynamics of objects and scenes captured in the video.

- Users can analyze the optical flow fields to understand motion trajectories, velocities, and patterns, enabling tasks such as object tracking, activity recognition, and scene understanding.

In summary, the GBBM algorithm with a Pyramid Approach leverages image pyramids to perform motion estimation at multiple resolutions, enhancing its ability to handle diverse motion dynamics in videos. By integrating information from different pyramid levels, the algorithm produces accurate and robust motion estimates, enabling detailed analysis and understanding of video content.

```python
def gradient_based_block_matching_pyramid(self, prev_frame_gray, frame_gray):
    # Initialize pyramid levels
    levels = int(self.level_entry.get())
    pyramid_prev = [prev_frame_gray]
    pyramid_frame = [frame_gray]
    for _ in range(levels - 1):
        prev_frame_gray = cv2.pyrDown(prev_frame_gray)
        frame_gray = cv2.pyrDown(frame_gray)
        pyramid_prev.append(prev_frame_gray)
        pyramid_frame.append(frame_gray)

    block_size = int(self.block_size_entry.get())  # Get block size from entry
    search_range = int(self.search_range_entry.get())  # Get search range from entry
    motion_vectors = np.zeros((frame_gray.shape[0] // block_size, frame_gray.shape[1] // block_size, 2))

    for level in range(levels - 1, -1, -1):  # Iterate over pyramid levels in reverse order
        prev_frame_gray = pyramid_prev[level]
        frame_gray = pyramid_frame[level]
        block_size = block_size * (2 ** level)  # Adjust block size based on pyramid level
        search_range = search_range * (2 ** level)  # Adjust search range based on pyramid level

        # Compute gradient of the previous frame
        grad_x_prev = cv2.Sobel(prev_frame_gray, cv2.CV_64F, 1, 0, ksize=3)
        grad_y_prev = cv2.Sobel(prev_frame_gray, cv2.CV_64F, 0, 1, ksize=3)

        for y in range(0, frame_gray.shape[0] - block_size, block_size):
            for x in range(0, frame_gray.shape[1] - block_size, block_size):
                min_cost = float('inf')
                best_dx = 0
                best_dy = 0
```

```
            for dy in range(-search_range, search_range + 1):
                for dx in range(-search_range, search_range + 1):
                    # Ensure the search area is within frame boundaries
                    if 0 <= y + dy < frame_gray.shape[0] - block_size and 0 <= x + dx < frame_gray.shape[1] - block_size:
                        template = prev_frame_gray[y:y+block_size, x:x+block_size]
                        search_area = frame_gray[y+dy:y+dy+block_size, x+dx:x+dx+block_size]

                        # Compute gradient of the search area
                        grad_x_search = cv2.Sobel(search_area, cv2.CV_64F, 1, 0, ksize=3)
                        grad_y_search = cv2.Sobel(search_area, cv2.CV_64F, 0, 1, ksize=3)

                        # Compute sum of squared differences of gradients
                        ssd_grad = np.sum((grad_x_prev[y:y+block_size, x:x+block_size] - grad_x_search)**2 + (grad_y_prev[y:y+block_size, x:x+block_size] - grad_y_search)**2)

                        if ssd_grad < min_cost:
                            min_cost = ssd_grad
                            best_dx = dx
                            best_dy = dy
                motion_vectors[y // block_size, x // block_size] = [best_dx, best_dy]

    return motion_vectors
```

Let's delve into each step of the Gradient-Based Block Matching (GBBM) algorithm with the Pyramid Approach:

1. Pyramid Initialization:

   The algorithm begins by creating image pyramids for both the previous and current frames. A pyramid is a multi-scale representation of an image, where each level corresponds to a different resolution. It starts with the original frame, and then each subsequent level is obtained by downsampling the previous level. This downsampling reduces the resolution of the image while preserving its essential features. The number of levels in the pyramid is determined by the levels parameter, which can be adjusted based on the desired trade-off between computational complexity and accuracy.

2. Parameter Scaling:

   As the algorithm operates at multiple resolutions, it scales certain parameters such as block size and search range to match the dimensions of each pyramid level. For example, a block size of 8x8 pixels at the highest resolution may correspond to a larger block size at lower resolutions. Similarly, the search range, which defines the spatial extent of the search for the best matching block, needs to be adjusted accordingly.

3. Gradient Calculation:

   At each pyramid level, the algorithm computes the gradients of the previous frame using the Sobel operator. Gradients provide information about the intensity variations in the image along the horizontal and vertical directions. These gradient images are used to measure the similarity between blocks during the block matching process.

4. Block Matching:

   Within each level of the pyramid, the algorithm performs block matching to estimate the motion vectors. Block matching involves comparing a block in the current frame with blocks in the previous frame to find the best match. This is typically done by minimizing a similarity metric, such as the sum of squared differences (SSD) between corresponding pixel values or gradients. The search for the best match is constrained within a specified search range around the block's location in the current frame.

5. Motion Vector Assignment:

   Once the best match for each block is found, the algorithm assigns a motion vector to represent the displacement between the corresponding blocks in the current and previous frames. These motion vectors capture the local motion patterns within the video sequence. By dividing the frame into blocks and estimating motion at each block, the algorithm can handle complex motion scenarios, including translation, rotation, and scaling.

6. Pyramid Integration:

   The block matching process is repeated for each level of the pyramid, with block sizes and search ranges adjusted accordingly. The motion vectors obtained from all pyramid levels are then integrated to produce the final set of motion vectors. This multi-scale approach allows the algorithm to capture motion information across different resolutions, effectively handling motion variations at different scales.

7. Result Return:

   Finally, the algorithm returns the computed motion vectors, which can be further analyzed or visualized to understand the motion dynamics of the video sequence. These motion vectors provide valuable insights into the temporal evolution of objects in the scene and can be used for various applications such as video compression, object tracking, and video stabilization.

By employing a pyramid-based approach and leveraging gradient information for block matching, the Gradient-Based Block Matching Algorithm with Pyramid Approach achieves robust and accurate motion estimation in videos, even in the presence of complex motion patterns and occlusions. It offers a balance between computational efficiency and motion estimation accuracy, making it suitable for real-time applications and video processing tasks.

RUNNING PROGRAM

Run program and click on Open Video button. Then, choose a video file then click on Next Frame button.

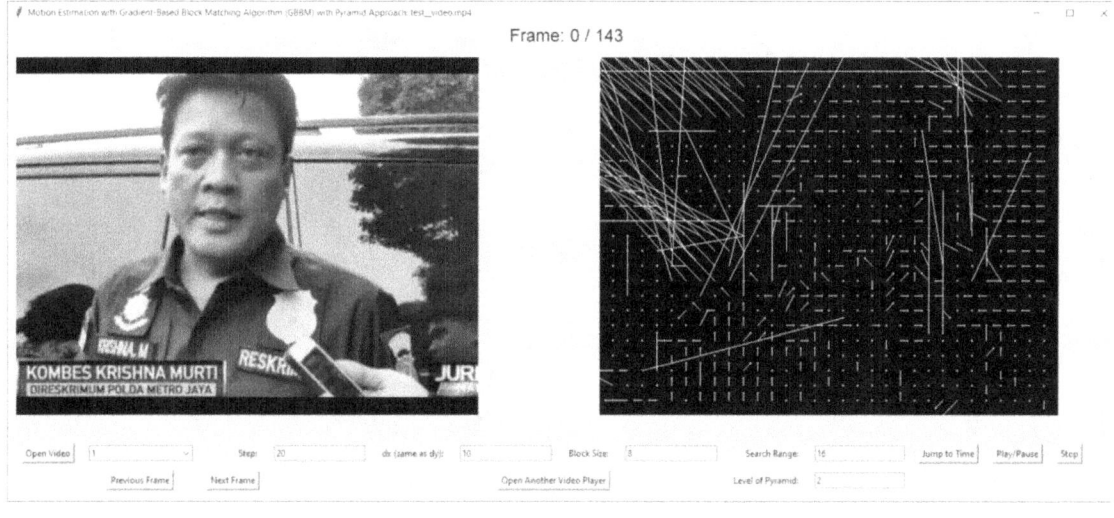

SOURCE CODE

```python
#gui_motion_analysis_gbbm_pyramid.py
import tkinter as tk
from tkinter import ttk
from tkinter import filedialog
from PIL import Image, ImageTk
import imageio
import cv2
import numpy as np

class VideoGBBM_Pyramid_OpticalFlow:
    def __init__(self, master):
        self.master = master
        self.master.title("Motion Estimation with Gradient-Based Block Matching Algorithm (GBBM) with Pyramid Approach")
        self.file_name = ""
        self.set_window_title()  # Set window title initially

        # Frame number label
        self.frame_number_label = tk.Label(master, text="Frame: 0")
        self.frame_number_label.pack()

        self.video = None
        self.video_path = None
        self.paused = False
        self.zoom_scale = tk.IntVar(value=1)
        self.frame_index = 0
        self.start_x1 = None
        self.start_y1 = None
        self.current_x1 = 0
        self.current_y1 = 0
        self.start_x2 = None
        self.start_y2 = None
        self.current_x2 = 0
        self.current_y2 = 0

        self.prev_frame_gray = None  # Initialize prev_frame_gray variable
        self.create_widgets()

    def create_widgets(self):
        # Panel for video display
        video_panel = tk.Frame(self.master)
        video_panel.pack(padx=10, pady=10)

        # Canvas to display the original video
        canvas_width = 800
```

```python
        canvas_height = 500
        self.canvas = tk.Canvas(video_panel, width=canvas_width, height=canvas_height)
        self.canvas.pack(side="left", fill="both", expand=True)
        self.canvas.bind("<MouseWheel>", self.on_mousewheel)
        self.canvas.bind("<ButtonPress-1>", self.on_press1)
        self.canvas.bind("<B1-Motion>", self.on_drag1)

        # Canvas to display the optical flow result
        self.flow_canvas = tk.Canvas(video_panel, width=canvas_width, height=canvas_height)
        self.flow_canvas.pack(side="right", fill="both", expand=True)
        self.flow_canvas.bind("<MouseWheel>", self.on_mousewheel)
        self.flow_canvas.bind("<ButtonPress-1>", self.on_press2)
        self.flow_canvas.bind("<B1-Motion>", self.on_drag2)

        # Panel for control buttons
        control_panel = tk.Frame(self.master)
        control_panel.pack(padx=10, pady=(0, 10), fill="x")

        # Button to open a video file
        self.open_button = tk.Button(control_panel, text="Open Video", command=self.open_video)
        self.open_button.grid(row=0, column=0, padx=10, pady=5)

        # Combobox for selecting zoom scale
        self.zoom_combobox = ttk.Combobox(control_panel, textvariable=self.zoom_scale, values=list(range(1, 11)))
        self.zoom_combobox.grid(row=0, column=1, padx=10, pady=5)
        self.zoom_combobox.bind("<<ComboboxSelected>>", self.update_zoom)

        # Label and entry for specifying step
        self.step_label = tk.Label(control_panel, text="Step:")
        self.step_label.grid(row=0, column=2, padx=10, pady=5, sticky="e")
        self.step_default = tk.StringVar(value="20")
        self.step_entry = ttk.Entry(control_panel, textvariable=self.step_default)
        self.step_entry.grid(row=0, column=3, padx=10, pady=5, sticky="w")
        self.step_entry.bind("<Return>", lambda event: self.toggle_play_pause())

        # Label and entry for specifying dx (same as dy)
        self.dx_label = tk.Label(control_panel, text="dx (same as dy):")
        self.dx_label.grid(row=0, column=4, padx=10, pady=5, sticky="e")
        self.dx_default = tk.StringVar(value="10")
        self.dx_entry = ttk.Entry(control_panel, textvariable=self.dx_default)
        self.dx_entry.grid(row=0, column=5, padx=10, pady=5, sticky="w")
        self.dx_entry.bind("<Return>", lambda event: self.toggle_play_pause())

        # Label and entry for specifying block size
```

```python
        self.block_size_label = tk.Label(control_panel, text="Block Size:")
        self.block_size_label.grid(row=0, column=6, padx=10, pady=5, sticky="e")
        self.block_size_default = tk.StringVar(value="8")
        self.block_size_entry = ttk.Entry(control_panel, textvariable=self.block_size_default)
        self.block_size_entry.grid(row=0, column=7, padx=10, pady=5, sticky="w")
        self.block_size_entry.bind("<Return>", lambda event: self.toggle_play_pause())

        # Label and entry for specifying search range
        self.search_range_label = tk.Label(control_panel, text="Search Range:")
        self.search_range_label.grid(row=0, column=8, padx=10, pady=5, sticky="e")
        self.search_range_default = tk.StringVar(value="16")
        self.search_range_entry = ttk.Entry(control_panel, textvariable=self.search_range_default)
        self.search_range_entry.grid(row=0, column=9, padx=10, pady=5, sticky="w")
        self.search_range_entry.bind("<Return>", lambda event: self.toggle_play_pause())

        # Button to jump to specified time
        self.jump_button = tk.Button(control_panel, text="Jump to Time", command=self.jump_to_time)
        self.jump_button.grid(row=0, column=10, padx=10, pady=5)

        # Button to play/pause the video
        self.play_button = tk.Button(control_panel, text="Play/Pause", command=self.toggle_play_pause)
        self.play_button.grid(row=0, column=11, padx=10, pady=5)

        # Button to stop the video
        self.stop_button = tk.Button(control_panel, text="Stop", command=self.stop_video)
        self.stop_button.grid(row=0, column=12, padx=10, pady=5)

        # Button to navigate to the previous frame
        self.prev_frame_button = tk.Button(control_panel, text="Previous Frame", command=self.prev_frame)
        self.prev_frame_button.grid(row=2, column=1, padx=10, pady=5)

        # Button to navigate to the next frame
        self.next_frame_button = tk.Button(control_panel, text="Next Frame", command=self.next_frame)
        self.next_frame_button.grid(row=2, column=2, padx=10, pady=5)

        # Button to open another instance of the application
        self.open_another_button = tk.Button(control_panel, text="Open Another Video Player", command=self.open_another_player)
```

```
            self.open_another_button.grid(row=2, column=0, columnspan=15, padx=10, pady=5)

        # Label and entry for specifying levels of pyramid
        self.level_label = tk.Label(control_panel, text="Level of Pyramid:")
        self.level_label.grid(row=2, column=8, padx=10, pady=5, sticky="e")
        self.level_default = tk.StringVar(value="2")
        self.level_entry = ttk.Entry(control_panel, textvariable=self.level_default)
        self.level_entry.grid(row=2, column=9, padx=10, pady=5, sticky="w")
        self.level_entry.bind("<Return>", lambda event: self.toggle_play_pause())

    def open_video(self):
        self.video_path = filedialog.askopenfilename(filetypes=[("Video files", "*.mp4;*.avi;*.mkv")])
        if self.video_path:
            self.video = imageio.get_reader(self.video_path)
            self.file_name = self.video_path.split('/')[-1]  # Extract file name
            self.set_window_title()  # Update window title with file name
            self.play_video()

    def play_video(self):
        if self.video:
            self.paused = False
            self.show_frame()
            self.show_optical_flow()

    def stop_video(self):
        self.paused = True
        self.frame_index = 0
        self.current_x1 = 0
        self.current_y1 = 0  # Reset the current position
        self.show_frame()
        self.show_optical_flow()

    def toggle_play_pause(self):
        self.paused = not self.paused
        if not self.paused:
            self.play_video()

    def update_zoom(self, event=None):
        self.show_frame()
        self.show_optical_flow()

    def show_frame(self):
        if self.video:
            if not self.paused:
                if 0 <= self.frame_index < len(self.video):  # Check if frame index is within range
```

```python
            try:
                frame = self.video.get_data(self.frame_index)
                frame_gray = cv2.cvtColor(frame, cv2.COLOR_RGB2GRAY)  # Convert to grayscale

                # Initialize prev_frame_gray on first frame
                if self.prev_frame_gray is None:
                    self.prev_frame_gray = frame_gray.copy()

                # Display current frame
                frame = Image.fromarray(frame)
                frame = frame.resize((frame.width * self.zoom_scale.get(), frame.height * self.zoom_scale.get()))
                photo = ImageTk.PhotoImage(frame)
                self.photo = photo  # Save object reference to PhotoImage globally

                self.canvas.delete("video")  # Delete previous image
                self.canvas.create_image(self.current_x1, self.current_y1, anchor="nw", image=photo, tags="video")

                # Update prev_frame_gray
                self.prev_frame_gray = frame_gray.copy()

                # Update frame number label
                self.frame_number_label.config(text=f"Frame: {self.frame_index} / {self.video.count_frames()}", font=("Helvetica", 18))

                self.frame_index += 1  # Move to the next frame

            except Exception as e:
                print("Error: ", e)

    def gradient_based_block_matching_pyramid(self, prev_frame_gray, frame_gray):
        # Initialize pyramid levels
        levels = int(self.level_entry.get())
        pyramid_prev = [prev_frame_gray]
        pyramid_frame = [frame_gray]
        for _ in range(levels - 1):
            prev_frame_gray = cv2.pyrDown(prev_frame_gray)
            frame_gray = cv2.pyrDown(frame_gray)
            pyramid_prev.append(prev_frame_gray)
            pyramid_frame.append(frame_gray)

        block_size = int(self.block_size_entry.get())  # Get block size from entry
        search_range = int(self.search_range_entry.get())  # Get search range from entry

        motion_vectors = np.zeros((frame_gray.shape[0] // block_size, frame_gray.shape[1] // block_size, 2))
```

```python
        for level in range(levels - 1, -1, -1):  # Iterate over pyramid levels in reverse order
            prev_frame_gray = pyramid_prev[level]
            frame_gray = pyramid_frame[level]
            block_size = block_size * (2 ** level)  # Adjust block size based on pyramid level
            search_range = search_range * (2 ** level)  # Adjust search range based on pyramid level

            # Compute gradient of the previous frame
            grad_x_prev = cv2.Sobel(prev_frame_gray, cv2.CV_64F, 1, 0, ksize=3)
            grad_y_prev = cv2.Sobel(prev_frame_gray, cv2.CV_64F, 0, 1, ksize=3)

            for y in range(0, frame_gray.shape[0] - block_size, block_size):
                for x in range(0, frame_gray.shape[1] - block_size, block_size):
                    min_cost = float('inf')
                    best_dx = 0
                    best_dy = 0
                    for dy in range(-search_range, search_range + 1):
                        for dx in range(-search_range, search_range + 1):
                            # Ensure the search area is within frame boundaries
                            if 0 <= y + dy < frame_gray.shape[0] - block_size and 0 <= x + dx < frame_gray.shape[1] - block_size:
                                template = prev_frame_gray[y:y+block_size, x:x+block_size]
                                search_area = frame_gray[y+dy:y+dy+block_size, x+dx:x+dx+block_size]

                                # Compute gradient of the search area
                                grad_x_search = cv2.Sobel(search_area, cv2.CV_64F, 1, 0, ksize=3)
                                grad_y_search = cv2.Sobel(search_area, cv2.CV_64F, 0, 1, ksize=3)

                                # Compute sum of squared differences of gradients
                                ssd_grad = np.sum((grad_x_prev[y:y+block_size, x:x+block_size] - grad_x_search)**2 + (grad_y_prev[y:y+block_size, x:x+block_size] - grad_y_search)**2)
                                if ssd_grad < min_cost:
                                    min_cost = ssd_grad
                                    best_dx = dx
                                    best_dy = dy
                    motion_vectors[y // block_size, x // block_size] = [best_dx, best_dy]

        return motion_vectors
```

```python
    def show_optical_flow(self):
        if self.video:
            if not self.paused:
                if 0 <= self.frame_index < len(self.video):  # Check if frame index is within range
                    try:
                        frame = self.video.get_data(self.frame_index)
                        frame_gray = cv2.cvtColor(frame, cv2.COLOR_RGB2GRAY)  # Convert to grayscale

                        # Calculate optical flow using Gradient-Based Block Matching Algorithm (GBBM)
                        motion_vectors = self.gradient_based_block_matching_pyramid(self.prev_frame_gray, frame_gray)

                        # Create an empty mask image for visualization
                        mask = np.zeros_like(frame)

                        # Compute flow visualization
                        step = int(self.step_entry.get())
                        for y in range(0, frame.shape[0], step):
                            for x in range(0, frame.shape[1], step):
                                # Ensure the motion vectors index does not exceed the bounds
                                if y // step < motion_vectors.shape[0] and x // step < motion_vectors.shape[1]:
                                    dx, dy = motion_vectors[y // step, x // step]

                                    # Scale the optical flow vectors
                                    dx *= int(self.dx_entry.get())
                                    dy *= int(self.dx_entry.get())
                                    # Convert coordinates to integers
                                    x1, y1 = int(x), int(y)
                                    x2, y2 = int(x + dx), int(y + dy)
                                    # Draw the line and circle
                                    cv2.line(mask, (x1, y1), (x2, y2), (255, 255, 255), 1)
                                    cv2.circle(mask, (x2, y2), 1, (0, 255, 0), -1)

                        # Convert mask to PIL format and display on canvas
                        mask = Image.fromarray(mask)
                        mask = ImageTk.PhotoImage(mask)
                        self.mask = mask
                        self.flow_canvas.delete("mask")  # Delete previous optical flow
                        self.flow_canvas.create_image(self.current_x2, self.current_y2, anchor="nw", image=mask, tags="mask")
```

```python
                    # Update previous frame
                    self.prev_frame_gray = frame_gray.copy()

            except Exception as e:
                print("Error in show_optical_flow:", e)  # Print error message

    def on_mousewheel(self, event):
        if event.delta > 0:
            self.zoom_scale.set(min(10, self.zoom_scale.get() + 1))
        else:
            self.zoom_scale.set(max(1, self.zoom_scale.get() - 1))

    def on_press1(self, event):
        self.start_x1 = event.x
        self.start_y1 = event.y

    def on_drag1(self, event):
        self.current_x1 += event.x - self.start_x1
        self.current_y1 += event.y - self.start_y1
        self.start_x1 = event.x
        self.start_y1 = event.y
        self.show_frame()

    def on_press2(self, event):
        self.start_x2 = event.x
        self.start_y2 = event.y

    def on_drag2(self, event):
        self.current_x2 += event.x - self.start_x2
        self.current_y2 += event.y - self.start_y2
        self.start_x2 = event.x
        self.start_y2 = event.y
        self.show_optical_flow()

    def jump_to_time(self):
        if self.video:
            try:
                time_in_seconds = float(self.step_entry.get())
                frame_number = int(time_in_seconds * self.video.get_meta_data()['fps'])
                self.frame_index = frame_number
                self.show_frame()
                self.show_optical_flow()
            except ValueError:
                print("Invalid time input.")

    def prev_frame(self):
```

```python
            if self.video:
                self.paused = True  # Pause video when manually navigating frames
                if self.frame_index > 0:
                    self.frame_index -= 1
                    self.show_frame()
                    self.show_optical_flow()

    def next_frame(self):
        if self.video:
            self.paused = True  # Pause video when manually navigating frames
            if self.frame_index < len(self.video) - 1:
                self.frame_index += 1
                self.show_frame()
                self.show_optical_flow()

    def set_window_title(self):
        self.master.title(f"Motion Estimation with Gradient-Based Block Matching 
Algorithm (GBBM) with Pyramid Approach: {self.file_name}")

    def open_another_player(self):
        root = tk.Tk()
        app = VideoGBBM_Pyramid_OpticalFlow(root)
        root.mainloop()

def main():
    root = tk.Tk()
    app = VideoGBBM_Pyramid_OpticalFlow(root)
    root.mainloop()

if __name__ == "__main__":
    main()
```

MOTION ESTIMATION WITH GRADIENT-BASED BLOCK MATCHING ALGORITHM (GBBM) WITH ADAPTIVE BLOCK SIZE

DESCRIPTION

The gui_motion_analysis_gbbm_adaptive.py script implements a graphical user interface (GUI) application for motion estimation in videos using the Gradient-Based Block Matching Algorithm (GBBM) with Adaptive Block Size. The application allows users to open video files, play/pause the video, navigate frame by frame, and visualize the optical flow (motion vectors) between consecutive frames. It offers interactive features such as zooming, panning, and jumping to specific time points within the video.

The GUI is built using the Tkinter library in Python, providing a user-friendly interface for interacting with video files and analyzing motion. Upon launching the application, users are presented with controls for opening video files, adjusting zoom scale, specifying motion estimation parameters such as step, block size, and search range, as well as buttons for controlling playback and navigation.

The main functionality of the application revolves around displaying the original video frames and visualizing the computed optical flow between frames. The optical flow is calculated using the GBBM algorithm with adaptive block size, which dynamically adjusts the block size based on the local gradient magnitude of the video frames. This adaptive approach improves the accuracy of motion estimation, particularly in regions with varying motion complexity.

The application leverages the PIL (Python Imaging Library) and OpenCV libraries to handle image processing tasks such as converting frames to grayscale, calculating gradients, and drawing motion vectors. It also utilizes the imageio library to read video files and extract individual frames for analysis.

Users can interact with the video display canvas to zoom in/out, pan across the video frames, and visualize the computed optical flow overlaid on the original frames. The application provides intuitive mouse and keyboard controls for these interactions, enhancing the user experience during motion analysis.

Overall, the gui_motion_analysis_gbbm_adaptive.py script serves as a versatile tool for motion analysis in videos, offering both visualization capabilities and parameter customization options to suit different use cases. It empowers users to gain insights into the motion dynamics of video sequences and supports various applications such as video compression, object tracking, and activity recognition.

IMPLEMENTING GRADIENT-BASED BLOCK MACHING WITH ADAPTIVE BLOCK SIZE

The Gradient-Based Block Matching with Adaptive Block Size (GBBM-ABS) is an extension of the traditional Block Matching Algorithm (BMA), a widely used technique for motion estimation in video processing. GBBM-ABS enhances the basic BMA by incorporating adaptive block size selection based on the local gradient magnitude of the video frames. Let's delve into the details of how GBBM-ABS works:
1. Block Matching Algorithm (BMA):

- BMA is a technique used to estimate motion vectors between consecutive frames in a video sequence.
- The basic idea involves dividing each frame into fixed-size blocks and searching for the best matching block in the subsequent frame by minimizing a predefined similarity metric, typically the Sum of Squared Differences (SSD) or Sum of Absolute Differences (SAD).
- Motion vectors represent the displacement between corresponding blocks in the current and reference frames, indicating the direction and magnitude of motion.

2. Gradient-Based Motion Estimation:
    - GBBM-ABS incorporates gradient information into the motion estimation process to improve accuracy, particularly in regions with varying motion complexity.
    - Instead of comparing pixel intensities directly, GBBM-ABS computes gradients (derivatives) of pixel intensities in both the reference and current frames.
    - Gradients provide information about the rate of change of intensity values, which can be more robust to variations in illumination, texture, and object boundaries.

3. Adaptive Block Size Selection:
    - The key innovation in GBBM-ABS is the adaptive selection of block sizes based on the local gradient magnitude of the video frames.
    - Rather than using a fixed block size for the entire frame, GBBM-ABS dynamically adjusts the block size according to the level of detail and motion complexity within each region.
    - Higher gradient magnitudes typically indicate areas with more significant motion or texture variations, requiring smaller block sizes for accurate motion estimation.
    - Lower gradient magnitudes correspond to smoother regions with less motion, where larger block sizes can be used without sacrificing accuracy.

4. Algorithm Workflow:
    - GBBM-ABS starts by computing gradients of pixel intensities in the reference frame (previous frame).
    - For each block in the current frame, an adaptive block size is determined based on the average gradient magnitude within the block.

- The algorithm then searches for the best matching block in the reference frame, considering a search range around the block's position.
- The similarity between blocks is evaluated based on the SSD or SAD of gradient magnitudes within corresponding regions.
- The motion vector corresponding to the block is calculated based on the displacement that minimizes the similarity metric.
- This process is repeated for all blocks in the frame, resulting in a set of motion vectors that describe the motion between consecutive frames.

5. Benefits and Applications:
   - GBBM-ABS improves the accuracy of motion estimation, particularly in scenarios with varying motion complexity and texture.
   - It enhances the robustness of motion estimation algorithms in real-world video processing applications such as video compression, object tracking, video stabilization, and activity recognition.

By adaptively adjusting block sizes based on local gradients, GBBM-ABS achieves better performance compared to traditional block matching techniques, especially in challenging environments with dynamic scenes and complex motion patterns.

```python
def gradient_based_block_matching_adaptive(self, prev_frame_gray, frame_gray):
    # GBBM implementation with adaptive block size
    search_range = int(self.search_range_entry.get())  # Get search range from entry
    block_size = int(self.block_size_entry.get())  # Get block size from entry
    motion_vectors = np.zeros((frame_gray.shape[0] // block_size, frame_gray.shape[1] // block_size, 2))

    # Compute gradient magnitude of the previous frame
    grad_x_search = cv2.Sobel(prev_frame_gray, cv2.CV_64F, 1, 0, ksize=3)
    grad_y_search = cv2.Sobel(prev_frame_gray, cv2.CV_64F, 0, 1, ksize=3)
    grad_mag_prev = np.sqrt(grad_x_search ** 2 + grad_y_search ** 2)

    for y in range(0, frame_gray.shape[0] - block_size + 1, block_size):
        for x in range(0, frame_gray.shape[1] - block_size + 1, block_size):
            # Calculate average gradient magnitude within the block
            block_grad_mag = grad_mag_prev[y:y+block_size, x:x+block_size]
            avg_grad_mag = np.mean(block_grad_mag)

            # Calculate adaptive block size based on average gradient magnitude
            adaptive_block_size = int(16 * (1 + avg_grad_mag / 255))  # Adjust the factor as needed
```

```
                min_cost = float('inf')
                best_dx = 0
                best_dy = 0
                for dy in range(-search_range, search_range + 1):
                    for dx in range(-search_range, search_range + 1):
                        # Ensure the search area is within block boundaries
                        if 0 <= y + dy < frame_gray.shape[0] - block_size and 0 <= x + dx < frame_gray.shape[1] - block_size:
                            grad_mag_search = np.sqrt(grad_x_search ** 2 + grad_y_search ** 2)

                            # Resize grad_mag_prev to match the size of the current block
                            grad_mag_search = cv2.resize(grad_mag_search, (block_size, block_size))

                            # Compute sum of squared differences of gradients
                            ssd_grad = np.sum((block_grad_mag - grad_mag_search) ** 2)

                            if ssd_grad < min_cost:
                                min_cost = ssd_grad
                                best_dx = dx
                                best_dy = dy
                motion_vectors[y // block_size, x // block_size] = [best_dx, best_dy]

    return motion_vectors
```

This gradient_based_block_matching_adaptive() function implements the Gradient-Based Block Matching with Adaptive Block Size (GBBM-ABS) algorithm for motion estimation between consecutive frames of a video sequence. Let's break down its functionality step by step:

1. Input Parameters:
   - prev_frame_gray: Grayscale representation of the previous frame.
   - frame_gray: Grayscale representation of the current frame.
2. Initialization:
   - Extracts the search range and block size parameters from the GUI entries.
   - Initializes an array motion_vectors to store the motion vectors for each block.
3. Compute Gradient Magnitude:
   - Computes the gradient magnitude of the previous frame using the Sobel operator.

- The Sobel operator calculates the gradient in the x and y directions, which are then combined to obtain the gradient magnitude.
- The gradient magnitude provides information about the rate of change of pixel intensities, helping to identify edges and regions of significant motion.

4. Block-wise Motion Estimation:
    - Iterates over each block in the current frame.
    - Calculates the average gradient magnitude within each block to determine its level of detail and motion complexity.
    - Computes an adaptive block size based on the average gradient magnitude. The adaptive block size is proportional to the magnitude, aiming to capture finer details in regions with higher gradients.
    - Performs a motion search within a local search range around the block's position in the previous frame.
    - For each candidate motion vector, computes the similarity between the current block and the corresponding search area in the previous frame.
    - Selects the motion vector that minimizes the sum of squared differences (SSD) of gradient magnitudes as the best match.
    - Stores the resulting motion vector in the motion_vectors array for further processing.

5. Output:

    Returns the motion_vectors array containing the motion vectors for each block in the current frame relative to the previous frame.

6. Remarks:
    - This adaptive approach improves the accuracy of motion estimation by adjusting the block size dynamically based on local image characteristics.
    - By considering the gradient magnitude, the algorithm can adapt to regions with varying motion complexity, leading to more reliable motion vectors.

The algorithm's performance may be influenced by parameters such as the search range, block size, and the factor used to scale the adaptive block size. Fine-tuning these parameters may be necessary to achieve optimal results in different scenarios.

RUNNING PROGRAM

Run program and click on Open Video button. Then, choose a video file then click on Next Frame button.

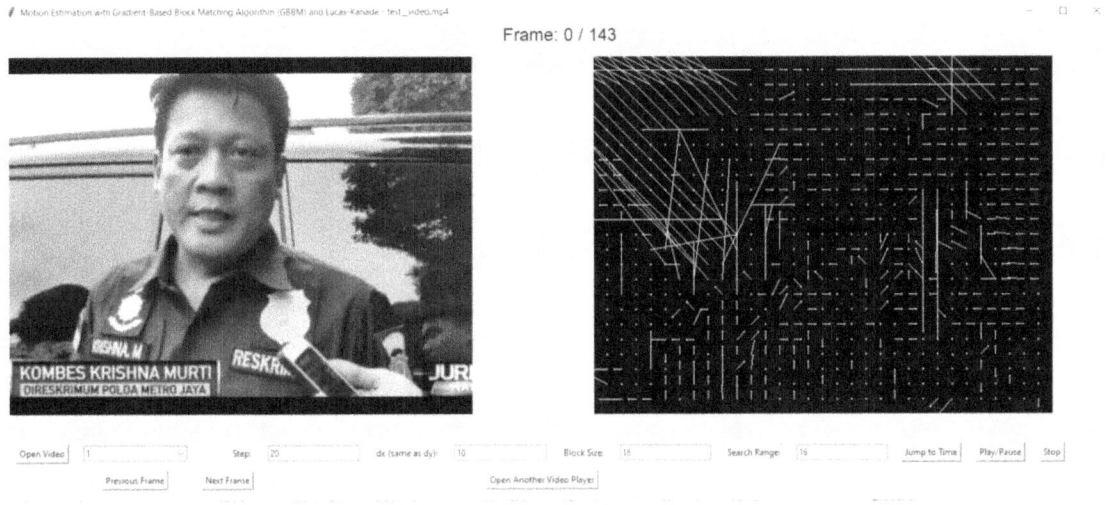

SOURCE CODE

```python
#gui_motion_analysis_gbbm_adaptive.py
import tkinter as tk
from tkinter import ttk
from tkinter import filedialog
from PIL import Image, ImageTk
import imageio
import cv2
import numpy as np

class VideoGBBMOpticalFlow:
    def __init__(self, master):
        self.master = master
        self.master.title("Motion Estimation with Gradient-Based Block Matching Algorithm (GBBM) with Adaptive Block Size")
        self.file_name = ""
        self.set_window_title()  # Set window title initially

        # Frame number label
        self.frame_number_label = tk.Label(master, text="Frame: 0")
        self.frame_number_label.pack()
```

```python
        self.video = None
        self.video_path = None
        self.paused = False
        self.zoom_scale = tk.IntVar(value=1)
        self.frame_index = 0
        self.start_x1 = None
        self.start_y1 = None
        self.current_x1 = 0
        self.current_y1 = 0
        self.start_x2 = None
        self.start_y2 = None
        self.current_x2 = 0
        self.current_y2 = 0

        self.prev_frame_gray = None  # Initialize prev_frame_gray variable
        self.create_widgets()

    def create_widgets(self):
        # Panel for video display
        video_panel = tk.Frame(self.master)
        video_panel.pack(padx=10, pady=10)

        # Canvas to display the original video
        canvas_width = 800
        canvas_height = 500
        self.canvas = tk.Canvas(video_panel, width=canvas_width, height=canvas_height)
        self.canvas.pack(side="left", fill="both", expand=True)
        self.canvas.bind("<MouseWheel>", self.on_mousewheel)
        self.canvas.bind("<ButtonPress-1>", self.on_press1)
        self.canvas.bind("<B1-Motion>", self.on_drag1)

        # Canvas to display the optical flow result
        self.flow_canvas = tk.Canvas(video_panel, width=canvas_width, height=canvas_height)
        self.flow_canvas.pack(side="right", fill="both", expand=True)
        self.flow_canvas.bind("<MouseWheel>", self.on_mousewheel)
        self.flow_canvas.bind("<ButtonPress-1>", self.on_press2)
        self.flow_canvas.bind("<B1-Motion>", self.on_drag2)

        # Panel for control buttons
        control_panel = tk.Frame(self.master)
        control_panel.pack(padx=10, pady=(0, 10), fill="x")

        # Button to open a video file
        self.open_button = tk.Button(control_panel, text="Open Video", command=self.open_video)
        self.open_button.grid(row=0, column=0, padx=10, pady=5)
```

```python
        # Combobox for selecting zoom scale
        self.zoom_combobox = ttk.Combobox(control_panel, 
textvariable=self.zoom_scale, values=list(range(1, 11)))
        self.zoom_combobox.grid(row=0, column=1, padx=10, pady=5)
        self.zoom_combobox.bind("<<ComboboxSelected>>", self.update_zoom)
        
        # Label and entry for specifying step
        self.step_label = tk.Label(control_panel, text="Step:")
        self.step_label.grid(row=0, column=2, padx=10, pady=5, sticky="e")
        self.step_default = tk.StringVar(value="20")
        self.step_entry = ttk.Entry(control_panel, textvariable=self.step_default)
        self.step_entry.grid(row=0, column=3, padx=10, pady=5, sticky="w")
        self.step_entry.bind("<Return>", lambda event: self.toggle_play_pause())
        
        # Label and entry for specifying dx (same as dy)
        self.dx_label = tk.Label(control_panel, text="dx (same as dy):")
        self.dx_label.grid(row=0, column=4, padx=10, pady=5, sticky="e")
        self.dx_default = tk.StringVar(value="10")
        self.dx_entry = ttk.Entry(control_panel, textvariable=self.dx_default)
        self.dx_entry.grid(row=0, column=5, padx=10, pady=5, sticky="w")
        self.dx_entry.bind("<Return>", lambda event: self.toggle_play_pause())
        
        # Label and entry for specifying block size
        self.block_size_label = tk.Label(control_panel, text="Block Size:")
        self.block_size_label.grid(row=0, column=6, padx=10, pady=5, sticky="e")
        self.block_size_default = tk.StringVar(value="8")
        self.block_size_entry = ttk.Entry(control_panel, 
textvariable=self.block_size_default)
        self.block_size_entry.grid(row=0, column=7, padx=10, pady=5, sticky="w")
        self.block_size_entry.bind("<Return>", lambda event: 
self.toggle_play_pause())
        
        # Label and entry for specifying search range
        self.search_range_label = tk.Label(control_panel, text="Search Range:")
        self.search_range_label.grid(row=0, column=8, padx=10, pady=5, sticky="e")
        self.search_range_default = tk.StringVar(value="4")
        self.search_range_entry = ttk.Entry(control_panel, 
textvariable=self.search_range_default)
        self.search_range_entry.grid(row=0, column=9, padx=10, pady=5, sticky="w")
        self.search_range_entry.bind("<Return>", lambda event: 
self.toggle_play_pause())
        
        # Button to jump to specified time
        self.jump_button = tk.Button(control_panel, text="Jump to Time", 
command=self.jump_to_time)
        self.jump_button.grid(row=0, column=10, padx=10, pady=5)
```

```python
        # Button to play/pause the video
        self.play_button = tk.Button(control_panel, text="Play/Pause", 
command=self.toggle_play_pause)
        self.play_button.grid(row=0, column=11, padx=10, pady=5)
        
        # Button to stop the video
        self.stop_button = tk.Button(control_panel, text="Stop", 
command=self.stop_video)
        self.stop_button.grid(row=0, column=12, padx=10, pady=5)

        # Button to navigate to the previous frame
        self.prev_frame_button = tk.Button(control_panel, text="Previous Frame", 
command=self.prev_frame)
        self.prev_frame_button.grid(row=2, column=1, padx=10, pady=5)
        
        # Button to navigate to the next frame
        self.next_frame_button = tk.Button(control_panel, text="Next Frame", 
command=self.next_frame)
        self.next_frame_button.grid(row=2, column=2, padx=10, pady=5)

        # Button to open another instance of the application
        self.open_another_button = tk.Button(control_panel, text="Open Another Video 
Player", command=self.open_another_player)
        self.open_another_button.grid(row=2, column=0, columnspan=15, padx=10, 
pady=5)

    def open_video(self):
        self.video_path = filedialog.askopenfilename(filetypes=[("Video files", 
"*.mp4;*.avi;*.mkv;*.wmv")])
        if self.video_path:
            self.video = imageio.get_reader(self.video_path)
            self.file_name = self.video_path.split('/')[-1]  # Extract file name
            self.set_window_title()  # Update window title with file name
            self.play_video()
    
    def play_video(self):
        if self.video:
            self.paused = False
            self.show_frame()
            self.show_optical_flow()

    def stop_video(self):
        self.paused = True
        self.frame_index = 0
        self.current_x1 = 0
        self.current_y1 = 0  # Reset the current position
        self.show_frame()
        self.show_optical_flow()
```

```python
    def toggle_play_pause(self):
        self.paused = not self.paused
        if not self.paused:
            self.play_video()

    def update_zoom(self, event=None):
        self.show_frame()
        self.show_optical_flow()

    def show_frame(self):
        if self.video:
            if not self.paused:
                if 0 <= self.frame_index < len(self.video):  # Check if frame index is within range
                    try:
                        frame = self.video.get_data(self.frame_index)
                        frame_gray = cv2.cvtColor(frame, cv2.COLOR_RGB2GRAY)  # Convert to grayscale

                        # Initialize prev_frame_gray on first frame
                        if self.prev_frame_gray is None:
                            self.prev_frame_gray = frame_gray.copy()

                        # Display current frame
                        frame = Image.fromarray(frame)
                        frame = frame.resize((frame.width * self.zoom_scale.get(), frame.height * self.zoom_scale.get()))
                        photo = ImageTk.PhotoImage(frame)
                        self.photo = photo  # Save object reference to PhotoImage globally
                        self.canvas.delete("video")  # Delete previous image
                        self.canvas.create_image(self.current_x1, self.current_y1, anchor="nw", image=photo, tags="video")

                        # Update prev_frame_gray
                        self.prev_frame_gray = frame_gray.copy()

                        # Update frame number label
                        self.frame_number_label.config(text=f"Frame: {self.frame_index} / {self.video.count_frames()}", font=("Helvetica", 18))

                        self.frame_index += 1  # Move to the next frame

                    except Exception as e:
                        print("Error: ", e)

    def gradient_based_block_matching_adaptive(self, prev_frame_gray, frame_gray):
```

```python
        # GBBM implementation with adaptive block size
        search_range = int(self.search_range_entry.get())  # Get search range from entry
        block_size = int(self.block_size_entry.get())  # Get block size from entry
        motion_vectors = np.zeros((frame_gray.shape[0] // block_size, frame_gray.shape[1] // block_size, 2))

        # Compute gradient magnitude of the previous frame
        grad_x_search = cv2.Sobel(prev_frame_gray, cv2.CV_64F, 1, 0, ksize=3)
        grad_y_search = cv2.Sobel(prev_frame_gray, cv2.CV_64F, 0, 1, ksize=3)
        grad_mag_prev = np.sqrt(grad_x_search ** 2 + grad_y_search ** 2)

        for y in range(0, frame_gray.shape[0] - block_size + 1, block_size):
            for x in range(0, frame_gray.shape[1] - block_size + 1, block_size):
                # Calculate average gradient magnitude within the block
                block_grad_mag = grad_mag_prev[y:y+block_size, x:x+block_size]
                avg_grad_mag = np.mean(block_grad_mag)

                # Calculate adaptive block size based on average gradient magnitude
                adaptive_block_size = int(16 * (1 + avg_grad_mag / 255))  # Adjust the factor as needed

                min_cost = float('inf')
                best_dx = 0
                best_dy = 0
                for dy in range(-search_range, search_range + 1):
                    for dx in range(-search_range, search_range + 1):
                        # Ensure the search area is within block boundaries
                        if 0 <= y + dy < frame_gray.shape[0] - block_size and 0 <= x + dx < frame_gray.shape[1] - block_size:
                            grad_mag_search = np.sqrt(grad_x_search ** 2 + grad_y_search ** 2)

                            # Resize grad_mag_prev to match the size of the current block
                            grad_mag_search = cv2.resize(grad_mag_search, (block_size, block_size))

                            # Compute sum of squared differences of gradients
                            ssd_grad = np.sum((block_grad_mag - grad_mag_search) ** 2)

                            if ssd_grad < min_cost:
                                min_cost = ssd_grad
                                best_dx = dx
                                best_dy = dy
                motion_vectors[y // block_size, x // block_size] = [best_dx, best_dy]
```

```python
        return motion_vectors


    def show_optical_flow(self):
        if self.video:
            if not self.paused:
                if 0 <= self.frame_index < len(self.video):  # Check if frame index is within range
                    try:
                        frame = self.video.get_data(self.frame_index)
                        frame_gray = cv2.cvtColor(frame, cv2.COLOR_RGB2GRAY)  # Convert to grayscale

                        # Calculate optical flow using Gradient-Based Block Matching Algorithm (GBBM) with adaptive block size
                        motion_vectors = self.gradient_based_block_matching_adaptive(self.prev_frame_gray, frame_gray)

                        # Create an empty mask image for visualization
                        mask = np.zeros_like(frame)

                        # Compute flow visualization
                        step = int(self.step_entry.get())
                        block_size = int(self.block_size_entry.get())  # Get block size
                        for y in range(0, frame.shape[0], step):
                            for x in range(0, frame.shape[1], step):
                                # Ensure the motion vectors index does not exceed the bounds
                                if y // step < motion_vectors.shape[0] and x // step < motion_vectors.shape[1]:
                                    dx, dy = motion_vectors[y // step, x // step]
                                    # Scale the optical flow vectors based on the zoom scale
                                    dx *= int(self.dx_entry.get())
                                    dy *= int(self.dx_entry.get())
                                    # Convert coordinates to integers
                                    x1, y1 = int(x), int(y)
                                    x2, y2 = int(x + dx), int(y + dy)

                                    # Draw the line and circle
                                    cv2.line(mask, (x1, y1), (x2, y2), (0, 255, 0), 1)

                                    cv2.circle(mask, (x2, y2), 1, (0, 255, 0), -1)

                        # Convert mask to PIL format and display on canvas
                        mask = Image.fromarray(mask)
                        mask = ImageTk.PhotoImage(mask)
```

```python
                        self.mask = mask
                        self.flow_canvas.delete("mask")  # Delete previous optical flow
                        self.flow_canvas.create_image(self.current_x2, self.current_y2, anchor="nw", image=mask, tags="mask")

                        # Update previous frame
                        self.prev_frame_gray = frame_gray.copy()

                except Exception as e:
                        print("Error in show_optical_flow:", e)  # Print error message

    def on_mousewheel(self, event):
        direction = event.delta // 120
        current_value = int(self.zoom_scale.get())
        if direction == 1 and current_value < 10:
            current_value += 1
        elif direction == -1 and current_value > 1:
            current_value -= 1
        self.zoom_scale.set(current_value)
        self.update_zoom()

    def on_press1(self, event):
        self.start_x1 = event.x
        self.start_y1 = event.y

    def on_drag1(self, event):
        if self.start_x1 and self.start_y1:
            self.x_offset1 = event.x - self.start_x1
            self.y_offset1 = event.y - self.start_y1
            self.current_x1 += self.x_offset1  # Update current position
            self.current_y1 += self.y_offset1  # Update current position
            self.canvas.move("video", self.x_offset1, self.y_offset1)
            self.start_x1 = event.x
            self.start_y1 = event.y

    def on_press2(self, event):
        self.start_x2 = event.x
        self.start_y2 = event.y

    def on_drag2(self, event):
        if self.start_x2 and self.start_y2:
            self.x_offset2 = event.x - self.start_x2
            self.y_offset2 = event.y - self.start_y2
            self.current_x2 += self.x_offset2  # Update current position
            self.current_y2 += self.y_offset2  # Update current position
```

```python
            self.flow_canvas.move("mask", self.x_offset2, self.y_offset2)  # Move optical flow canvas along with original canvas
            self.start_x2 = event.x
            self.start_y2 = event.y

    def jump_to_time(self):
        time_str = self.time_entry.get()
        try:
            time_seconds = float(time_str)
            if 0 <= time_seconds:
                self.frame_index = int(time_seconds * self.video.get_meta_data()['fps'])
                self.show_frame()
                self.show_optical_flow()  # Jump to specified time for optical flow
        except ValueError:
            pass
    def prev_frame(self):
        if self.frame_index > 0:
            self.frame_index -= 1
            self.show_frame()
            self.show_optical_flow()
            print(self.frame_index)
    def next_frame(self):
        if self.video and self.frame_index < len(self.video) - 1:
            self.show_frame()
            self.show_optical_flow()
            print(self.frame_index)
    def set_window_title(self):
        if self.file_name:
            self.master.title(f"Motion Estimation with Gradient-Based Block Matching Algorithm (GBBM) - {self.file_name}")
            self.master.title_font = ("Helvetica", 16, "bold")
        else:
            self.master.title("Motion Estimation with Gradient-Based Block Matching Algorithm (GBBM)")

    def open_another_player(self):
        # Open another instance of the application
        root = tk.Toplevel(self.master)
        app = VideoGBBMOpticalFlow(root)

def main():
    root = tk.Tk()
    app = VideoGBBMOpticalFlow(root)
    root.mainloop()

if __name__ == "__main__":
    main()
```

COMBINING MOTION ESTIMATION WITH GRADIENT-BASED BLOCK MATCHING ALGORITHM (GBBM) AND LUCAS-KANADE

DESCRIPTION

This Python script, gui_motion_analysis_gbbm_lucas_kanade.py, implements a graphical user interface (GUI) for motion estimation in videos using the Gradient-Based Block Matching Algorithm (GBBM) and Lucas-Kanade Optical Flow. Let's break down its structure and functionality:

The script begins with importing necessary libraries, including tkinter for GUI development, PIL for image processing, imageio for reading video files, cv2 for computer vision operations, and numpy for numerical computation.

The VideoGBBM_LK_OpticalFlow class is defined, serving as the main application container. It initializes various attributes such as window title, file name, video parameters, and GUI elements.

The create_widgets method sets up the layout of the GUI, including panels for video display, control buttons, and entry fields for setting parameters like zoom scale, step, dx (change in x direction), block size, and search range.

Methods like open_video, play_video, toggle_play_pause, update_zoom, show_frame, and show_optical_flow handle video loading, playback control, zooming, frame display, and optical flow visualization.

The script provides implementations for two methods for computing optical flow: gradient_based_block_matching for GBBM and lucas_kanade_optical_flow for Lucas-Kanade method. These methods calculate motion vectors for each block in consecutive frames.

The on_mousewheel, on_press1, on_drag1, on_press2, and on_drag2 methods handle events such as mouse wheel scrolling and dragging for panning the video display and optical flow visualization.

Additional functionality includes jumping to a specific time in the video, navigating between frames, setting window title, and opening multiple instances of the application.

Finally, the main function creates the main application window and starts the event loop.

Overall, this script provides a user-friendly interface for visualizing and analyzing motion in videos using two different optical flow estimation techniques.

IMPLEMENTING GRADIENT-BASED BLOCK MACHING AND LUCAS-KANADE

```
def lucas_kanade_optical_flow(self, prev_frame_gray, frame_gray):
    # Lucas-Kanade Optical Flow implementation
    block_size = int(self.block_size_entry.get())  # Get block size from entry
```

```python
        motion_vectors = np.zeros((frame_gray.shape[0] // block_size,
frame_gray.shape[1] // block_size, 2))

        # Parameters for Lucas-Kanade method
        lk_params = dict(winSize=(block_size, block_size), maxLevel=2,
criteria=(cv2.TERM_CRITERIA_EPS | cv2.TERM_CRITERIA_COUNT, 10, 0.03))

        # Find corners in the previous frame
        prev_corners = cv2.goodFeaturesToTrack(prev_frame_gray, maxCorners=100,
qualityLevel=0.01, minDistance=10, blockSize=block_size)

        # Calculate optical flow for each corner
        if prev_corners is not None:
            next_corners, status, _ = cv2.calcOpticalFlowPyrLK(prev_frame_gray,
frame_gray, prev_corners, None, **lk_params)

            # Filter valid optical flow vectors
            good_new = next_corners[status == 1]
            good_old = prev_corners[status == 1]

            # Compute motion vectors
            for i, (new, old) in enumerate(zip(good_new, good_old)):
                old_x, old_y = old.ravel()
                new_x, new_y = new.ravel()
                dx = new_x - old_x
                dy = new_y - old_y
                motion_vectors[int(old_y / block_size), int(old_x / block_size)] =
[dx, dy]

        return motion_vectors
```

This lucas_kanade_optical_flow method implements the Lucas-Kanade Optical Flow algorithm for estimating motion vectors between consecutive frames of a video. Let's go through its functionality step by step:

1. Block Size Determination: It starts by retrieving the block size from the GUI entry field, which allows the user to specify the size of blocks to use for motion estimation.
2. Initialization: It initializes a numpy array to store the motion vectors. The size of this array is determined by dividing the dimensions of the frame by the block size, resulting in a grid of blocks over the frame.
3. Parameter Configuration: It sets up parameters required for the Lucas-Kanade method. This includes the window size (winSize) for the optical flow algorithm, the maximum pyramid level (maxLevel) for the image pyramid, and termination criteria (criteria) to determine when to stop the iterative process.

4. Feature Detection: It uses the cv2.goodFeaturesToTrack function to detect corners in the previous frame (prev_frame_gray). This function identifies key points that are likely to remain visible in subsequent frames.
5. Optical Flow Computation: It computes the optical flow for each detected corner using the cv2.calcOpticalFlowPyrLK function. This function tracks the movement of these corners from the previous frame to the current frame.
6. Filtering: It filters out invalid optical flow vectors based on the status returned by the cv2.calcOpticalFlowPyrLK function. Only vectors corresponding to successfully tracked corners are considered.
7. Motion Vector Calculation: It calculates the motion vectors by subtracting the coordinates of the detected corners in the previous frame from their corresponding coordinates in the current frame.
8. Storing Motion Vectors: It stores the computed motion vectors in the motion_vectors array at positions corresponding to the blocks in the grid.
9. Return: Finally, it returns the motion_vectors array containing the estimated motion vectors for each block in the frame.

This method effectively implements the Lucas-Kanade Optical Flow algorithm, providing a means to estimate motion between frames, which is essential for various computer vision tasks such as tracking objects and analyzing motion patterns.

SHOWING OPTICAL FLOW

```
def show_optical_flow(self):
    if self.video:
        if not self.paused:
            if 0 <= self.frame_index < len(self.video):  # Check if frame index is within range
                try:
                    frame = self.video.get_data(self.frame_index)
                    frame_gray = cv2.cvtColor(frame, cv2.COLOR_RGB2GRAY)  # Convert to grayscale

                    # Calculate optical flow using Gradient-Based Block Matching Algorithm (GBBM)
                    motion_vectors_gbbm = self.gradient_based_block_matching(self.prev_frame_gray, frame_gray)

                    # Calculate optical flow using Lucas-Kanade method
```

```python
                    motion_vectors_lk = 
self.lucas_kanade_optical_flow(self.prev_frame_gray, frame_gray)

                    # Combine optical flow results
                    motion_vectors_combined = motion_vectors_gbbm + 
motion_vectors_lk

                    # Create an empty mask image for visualization
                    mask = np.zeros_like(frame)

                    # Compute flow visualization
                    step = int(self.step_entry.get())
                    for y in range(0, frame.shape[0], step):
                        for x in range(0, frame.shape[1], step):
                            # Ensure the motion vectors index does not exceed the 
bounds
                            if y // step < motion_vectors_combined.shape[0] and x 
// step < motion_vectors_combined.shape[1]:
                                dx, dy = motion_vectors_combined[y // step, x // 
step]
                                # Scale the optical flow vectors based on the 
zoom scale
                                dx *= int(self.dx_entry.get())
                                dy *= int(self.dx_entry.get())
                                # Convert coordinates to integers
                                x1, y1 = int(x), int(y)
                                x2, y2 = int(x + dx), int(y + dy)
                                # Draw the line and circle
                                cv2.line(mask, (x1, y1), (x2, y2), (255, 255, 
255), 1)
                                cv2.circle(mask, (x2, y2), 1, (0, 255, 0), -1)

                    # Convert mask to PIL format and display on canvas
                    mask = Image.fromarray(mask)
                    mask = ImageTk.PhotoImage(mask)
                    self.mask = mask
                    self.flow_canvas.delete("mask")   # Delete previous optical 
flow
                    self.flow_canvas.create_image(self.current_x2, 
self.current_y2, anchor="nw", image=mask, tags="mask")

                    #self.frame_index += 1  # Move to the next frame

                    # Update previous frame
                    self.prev_frame_gray = frame_gray.copy()

            except Exception as e:
```

```
            print("Error in show_optical_flow:", e)  # Print error
message
```

The show_optical_flow() method is responsible for visualizing the optical flow computed using two different methods: Gradient-Based Block Matching (GBBM) Algorithm and Lucas-Kanade method. Let's break down its functionality:

1. Video Playback Check: It first checks if a video is loaded (self.video) and if the video is not paused. If both conditions are met, it proceeds to process the frames.
2. Frame Index Range Check: It ensures that the current frame index is within the range of the video frames.
3. Frame Acquisition and Grayscale Conversion: It retrieves the current frame using self.video.get_data(self.frame_index) and converts it to grayscale using OpenCV's cv2.cvtColor function.
4. Optical Flow Computation: It computes the optical flow using both the Gradient-Based Block Matching (GBBM) Algorithm and the Lucas-Kanade method by calling their respective functions (self.gradient_based_block_matching and self.lucas_kanade_optical_flow). This results in two sets of motion vectors.
5. Combining Optical Flow Results: It combines the results from both methods by adding their corresponding motion vectors together.
6. Flow Visualization: It visualizes the combined optical flow on a blank image. It iterates through the motion vectors and draws lines and circles on the blank image to represent the flow. The step parameter controls the spacing between vectors. The dx and dy values are scaled based on the zoom scale (self.dx_entry.get()), and then converted to integer coordinates for drawing.
7. Conversion and Display: It converts the resulting image (mask) to a PIL format and then to an ImageTk.PhotoImage object for display on the canvas (self.flow_canvas). The previous optical flow visualization is deleted, and the new one is created at the current position (self.current_x2, self.current_y2).
8. Error Handling: It catches any exceptions that occur during the process and prints an error message.

This method effectively visualizes the computed optical flow on the canvas, providing a visual representation of motion between frames in the video.

RUNNING PROGRAM

Run program and click on Open Video button. Then, choose a video file then click on Next Frame button.

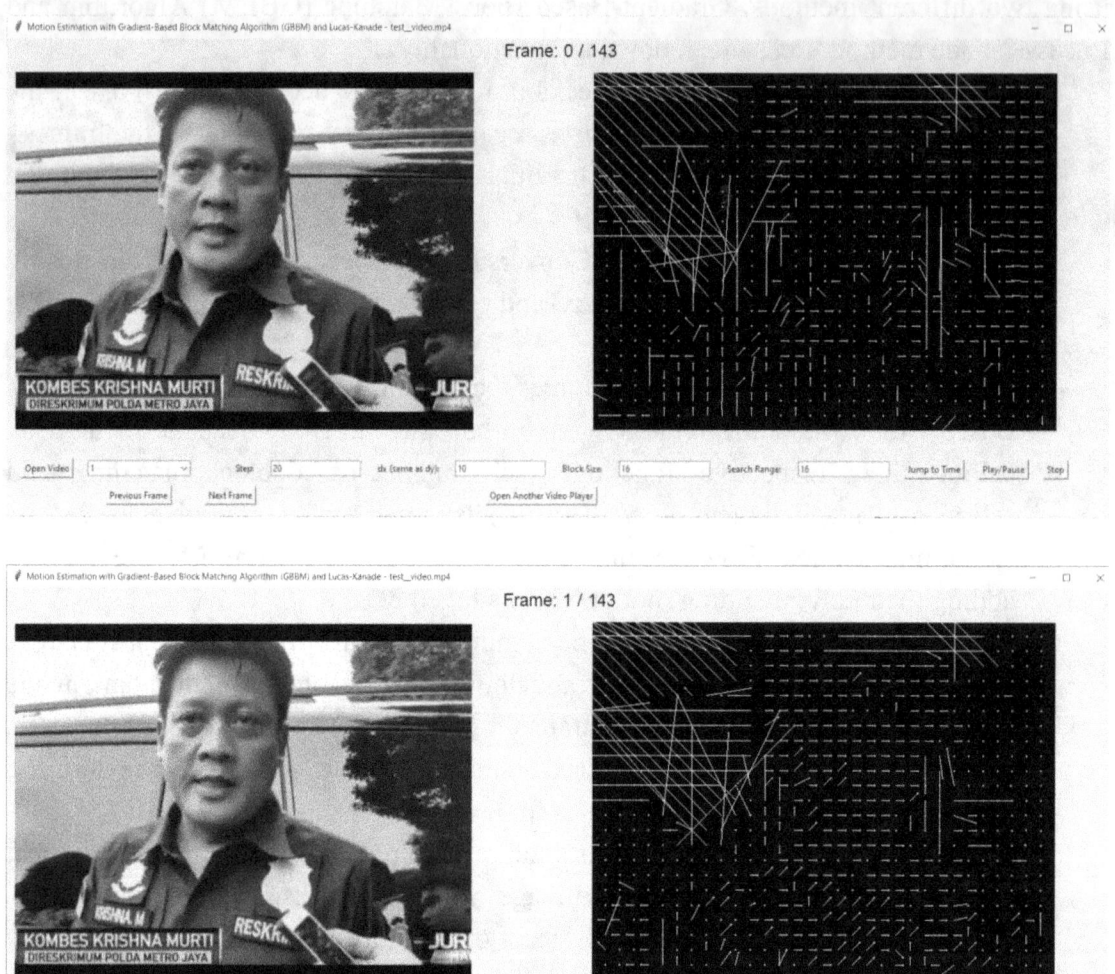

SOURCE CODE

```python
#gui_motion_analysis_gbbm_lucas_kanade.py
import tkinter as tk
from tkinter import ttk
from tkinter import filedialog
from PIL import Image, ImageTk
import imageio
import cv2
import numpy as np

class VideoGBBM_LK_OpticalFlow:
    def __init__(self, master):
        self.master = master
        self.master.title("Motion Estimation with Gradient-Based Block Matching Algorithm (GBBM) and Lucas-Kanade")
        self.file_name = ""
        self.set_window_title()  # Set window title initially

        # Frame number label
        self.frame_number_label = tk.Label(master, text="Frame: 0")
        self.frame_number_label.pack()

        self.video = None
        self.video_path = None
        self.paused = False
        self.zoom_scale = tk.IntVar(value=1)
        self.frame_index = 0
        self.start_x1 = None
        self.start_y1 = None
        self.current_x1 = 0
        self.current_y1 = 0
        self.start_x2 = None
        self.start_y2 = None
        self.current_x2 = 0
        self.current_y2 = 0

        self.prev_frame_gray = None  # Initialize prev_frame_gray variable
        self.create_widgets()

    def create_widgets(self):
        # Panel for video display
        video_panel = tk.Frame(self.master)
        video_panel.pack(padx=10, pady=10)

        # Canvas to display the original video
        canvas_width = 800
```

```python
        canvas_height = 500
        self.canvas = tk.Canvas(video_panel, width=canvas_width, height=canvas_height)
        self.canvas.pack(side="left", fill="both", expand=True)
        self.canvas.bind("<MouseWheel>", self.on_mousewheel)
        self.canvas.bind("<ButtonPress-1>", self.on_press1)
        self.canvas.bind("<B1-Motion>", self.on_drag1)

        # Canvas to display the optical flow result
        self.flow_canvas = tk.Canvas(video_panel, width=canvas_width, height=canvas_height)
        self.flow_canvas.pack(side="right", fill="both", expand=True)
        self.flow_canvas.bind("<MouseWheel>", self.on_mousewheel)
        self.flow_canvas.bind("<ButtonPress-1>", self.on_press2)
        self.flow_canvas.bind("<B1-Motion>", self.on_drag2)

        # Panel for control buttons
        control_panel = tk.Frame(self.master)
        control_panel.pack(padx=10, pady=(0, 10), fill="x")

        # Button to open a video file
        self.open_button = tk.Button(control_panel, text="Open Video", command=self.open_video)
        self.open_button.grid(row=0, column=0, padx=10, pady=5)

        # Combobox for selecting zoom scale
        self.zoom_combobox = ttk.Combobox(control_panel, textvariable=self.zoom_scale, values=list(range(1, 11)))
        self.zoom_combobox.grid(row=0, column=1, padx=10, pady=5)
        self.zoom_combobox.bind("<<ComboboxSelected>>", self.update_zoom)

        # Label and entry for specifying step
        self.step_label = tk.Label(control_panel, text="Step:")
        self.step_label.grid(row=0, column=2, padx=10, pady=5, sticky="e")
        self.step_default = tk.StringVar(value="20")
        self.step_entry = ttk.Entry(control_panel, textvariable=self.step_default)
        self.step_entry.grid(row=0, column=3, padx=10, pady=5, sticky="w")
        self.step_entry.bind("<Return>", lambda event: self.toggle_play_pause())

        # Label and entry for specifying dx (same as dy)
        self.dx_label = tk.Label(control_panel, text="dx (same as dy):")
        self.dx_label.grid(row=0, column=4, padx=10, pady=5, sticky="e")
        self.dx_default = tk.StringVar(value="10")
        self.dx_entry = ttk.Entry(control_panel, textvariable=self.dx_default)
        self.dx_entry.grid(row=0, column=5, padx=10, pady=5, sticky="w")
        self.dx_entry.bind("<Return>", lambda event: self.toggle_play_pause())

        # Label and entry for specifying block size
```

```python
        self.block_size_label = tk.Label(control_panel, text="Block Size:")
        self.block_size_label.grid(row=0, column=6, padx=10, pady=5, sticky="e")
        self.block_size_default = tk.StringVar(value="16")
        self.block_size_entry = ttk.Entry(control_panel, textvariable=self.block_size_default)
        self.block_size_entry.grid(row=0, column=7, padx=10, pady=5, sticky="w")
        self.block_size_entry.bind("<Return>", lambda event: self.toggle_play_pause())

        # Label and entry for specifying search range
        self.search_range_label = tk.Label(control_panel, text="Search Range:")
        self.search_range_label.grid(row=0, column=8, padx=10, pady=5, sticky="e")
        self.search_range_default = tk.StringVar(value="16")
        self.search_range_entry = ttk.Entry(control_panel, textvariable=self.search_range_default)
        self.search_range_entry.grid(row=0, column=9, padx=10, pady=5, sticky="w")
        self.search_range_entry.bind("<Return>", lambda event: self.toggle_play_pause())

        # Button to jump to specified time
        self.jump_button = tk.Button(control_panel, text="Jump to Time", command=self.jump_to_time)
        self.jump_button.grid(row=0, column=10, padx=10, pady=5)

        # Button to play/pause the video
        self.play_button = tk.Button(control_panel, text="Play/Pause", command=self.toggle_play_pause)
        self.play_button.grid(row=0, column=11, padx=10, pady=5)

        # Button to stop the video
        self.stop_button = tk.Button(control_panel, text="Stop", command=self.stop_video)
        self.stop_button.grid(row=0, column=12, padx=10, pady=5)

        # Button to navigate to the previous frame
        self.prev_frame_button = tk.Button(control_panel, text="Previous Frame", command=self.prev_frame)
        self.prev_frame_button.grid(row=2, column=1, padx=10, pady=5)

        # Button to navigate to the next frame
        self.next_frame_button = tk.Button(control_panel, text="Next Frame", command=self.next_frame)
        self.next_frame_button.grid(row=2, column=2, padx=10, pady=5)

        # Button to open another instance of the application
        self.open_another_button = tk.Button(control_panel, text="Open Another Video Player", command=self.open_another_player)
```

```python
        self.open_another_button.grid(row=2, column=0, columnspan=15, padx=10, pady=5)

    def open_video(self):
        self.video_path = filedialog.askopenfilename(filetypes=[("Video files", "*.mp4;*.avi;*.mkv")])
        if self.video_path:
            self.video = imageio.get_reader(self.video_path)
            self.file_name = self.video_path.split('/')[-1]  # Extract file name
            self.set_window_title()  # Update window title with file name
            self.play_video()

    def play_video(self):
        if self.video:
            self.paused = False
            self.show_frame()
            self.show_optical_flow()

    def stop_video(self):
        self.paused = True
        self.frame_index = 0
        self.current_x1 = 0
        self.current_y1 = 0  # Reset the current position
        self.show_frame()
        self.show_optical_flow()

    def toggle_play_pause(self):
        self.paused = not self.paused
        if not self.paused:
            self.play_video()

    def update_zoom(self, event=None):
        self.show_frame()
        self.show_optical_flow()

    def show_frame(self):
        if self.video:
            if not self.paused:
                if 0 <= self.frame_index < len(self.video):  # Check if frame index is within range
                    try:
                        frame = self.video.get_data(self.frame_index)
                        frame_gray = cv2.cvtColor(frame, cv2.COLOR_RGB2GRAY)  # Convert to grayscale

                        # Initialize prev_frame_gray on first frame
                        if self.prev_frame_gray is None:
                            self.prev_frame_gray = frame_gray.copy()
```

```python
                        # Display current frame
                        frame = Image.fromarray(frame)
                        frame = frame.resize((frame.width * self.zoom_scale.get(), 
frame.height * self.zoom_scale.get()))
                        photo = ImageTk.PhotoImage(frame)
                        self.photo = photo  # Save object reference to PhotoImage 
globally
                        self.canvas.delete("video")  # Delete previous image
                        self.canvas.create_image(self.current_x1, self.current_y1, 
anchor="nw", image=photo, tags="video")

                        # Update prev_frame_gray
                        self.prev_frame_gray = frame_gray.copy()

                        # Update frame number label
                        self.frame_number_label.config(text=f"Frame: 
{self.frame_index} / {self.video.count_frames()}", font=("Helvetica", 18))

                        self.frame_index += 1  # Move to the next frame

                except Exception as e:
                    print("Error: ", e)

    def gradient_based_block_matching(self, prev_frame_gray, frame_gray):
        # GBBM implementation
        block_size = int(self.block_size_entry.get())  # Get block size from entry
        search_range = int(self.search_range_entry.get())  # Get search range from 
entry
        motion_vectors = np.zeros((frame_gray.shape[0] // block_size, 
frame_gray.shape[1] // block_size, 2))

        # Compute gradient of the previous frame
        grad_x_prev = cv2.Sobel(prev_frame_gray, cv2.CV_64F, 1, 0, ksize=3)
        grad_y_prev = cv2.Sobel(prev_frame_gray, cv2.CV_64F, 0, 1, ksize=3)

        for y in range(0, frame_gray.shape[0] - block_size, block_size):
            for x in range(0, frame_gray.shape[1] - block_size, block_size):
                min_cost = float('inf')
                best_dx = 0
                best_dy = 0
                for dy in range(-search_range, search_range + 1):
                    for dx in range(-search_range, search_range + 1):
                        # Ensure the search area is within frame boundaries
                        if 0 <= y + dy < frame_gray.shape[0] - block_size and 0 <= x 
+ dx < frame_gray.shape[1] - block_size:
                            template = prev_frame_gray[y:y+block_size, 
x:x+block_size]
```

```python
                            search_area = frame_gray[y+dy:y+dy+block_size, x+dx:x+dx+block_size]

                            # Compute gradient of the search area
                            grad_x_search = cv2.Sobel(search_area, cv2.CV_64F, 1, 0, ksize=3)
                            grad_y_search = cv2.Sobel(search_area, cv2.CV_64F, 0, 1, ksize=3)

                            # Compute sum of squared differences of gradients
                            ssd_grad = np.sum((grad_x_prev[y:y+block_size, x:x+block_size] - grad_x_search)**2 + (grad_y_prev[y:y+block_size, x:x+block_size] - grad_y_search)**2)
                            if ssd_grad < min_cost:
                                min_cost = ssd_grad
                                best_dx = dx
                                best_dy = dy
                    motion_vectors[y // block_size, x // block_size] = [best_dx, best_dy]

        return motion_vectors

    def lucas_kanade_optical_flow(self, prev_frame_gray, frame_gray):
        # Lucas-Kanade Optical Flow implementation
        block_size = int(self.block_size_entry.get())  # Get block size from entry
        motion_vectors = np.zeros((frame_gray.shape[0] // block_size, frame_gray.shape[1] // block_size, 2))

        # Parameters for Lucas-Kanade method
        lk_params = dict(winSize=(block_size, block_size), maxLevel=2, criteria=(cv2.TERM_CRITERIA_EPS | cv2.TERM_CRITERIA_COUNT, 10, 0.03))

        # Find corners in the previous frame
        prev_corners = cv2.goodFeaturesToTrack(prev_frame_gray, maxCorners=100, qualityLevel=0.01, minDistance=10, blockSize=block_size)

        # Calculate optical flow for each corner
        if prev_corners is not None:
            next_corners, status, _ = cv2.calcOpticalFlowPyrLK(prev_frame_gray, frame_gray, prev_corners, None, **lk_params)

            # Filter valid optical flow vectors
            good_new = next_corners[status == 1]
            good_old = prev_corners[status == 1]

            # Compute motion vectors
            for i, (new, old) in enumerate(zip(good_new, good_old)):
                old_x, old_y = old.ravel()
                new_x, new_y = new.ravel()
```

```python
                    dx = new_x - old_x
                    dy = new_y - old_y
                    motion_vectors[int(old_y / block_size), int(old_x / block_size)] = [dx, dy]

        return motion_vectors

    def show_optical_flow(self):
        if self.video:
            if not self.paused:
                if 0 <= self.frame_index < len(self.video):  # Check if frame index is within range
                    try:
                        frame = self.video.get_data(self.frame_index)
                        frame_gray = cv2.cvtColor(frame, cv2.COLOR_RGB2GRAY)  # Convert to grayscale

                        # Calculate optical flow using Gradient-Based Block Matching Algorithm (GBBM)
                        motion_vectors_gbbm = self.gradient_based_block_matching(self.prev_frame_gray, frame_gray)

                        # Calculate optical flow using Lucas-Kanade method
                        motion_vectors_lk = self.lucas_kanade_optical_flow(self.prev_frame_gray, frame_gray)

                        # Combine optical flow results
                        motion_vectors_combined = motion_vectors_gbbm + motion_vectors_lk

                        # Create an empty mask image for visualization
                        mask = np.zeros_like(frame)

                        # Compute flow visualization
                        step = int(self.step_entry.get())
                        for y in range(0, frame.shape[0], step):
                            for x in range(0, frame.shape[1], step):
                                # Ensure the motion vectors index does not exceed the bounds
                                if y // step < motion_vectors_combined.shape[0] and x // step < motion_vectors_combined.shape[1]:
                                    dx, dy = motion_vectors_combined[y // step, x // step]
                                    # Scale the optical flow vectors based on the zoom scale
                                    dx *= int(self.dx_entry.get())
                                    dy *= int(self.dx_entry.get())
                                    # Convert coordinates to integers
```

```python
                            x1, y1 = int(x), int(y)
                            x2, y2 = int(x + dx), int(y + dy)
                            # Draw the line and circle
                            cv2.line(mask, (x1, y1), (x2, y2), (255, 255, 255), 1)

                            cv2.circle(mask, (x2, y2), 1, (0, 255, 0), -1)

                    # Convert mask to PIL format and display on canvas
                    mask = Image.fromarray(mask)
                    mask = ImageTk.PhotoImage(mask)
                    self.mask = mask
                    self.flow_canvas.delete("mask")  # Delete previous optical flow
                    self.flow_canvas.create_image(self.current_x2, self.current_y2, anchor="nw", image=mask, tags="mask")

                    #self.frame_index += 1  # Move to the next frame

                    # Update previous frame
                    self.prev_frame_gray = frame_gray.copy()

            except Exception as e:
                print("Error in show_optical_flow:", e)  # Print error message

    def on_mousewheel(self, event):
        direction = event.delta // 120
        current_value = int(self.zoom_scale.get())
        if direction == 1 and current_value < 10:
            current_value += 1
        elif direction == -1 and current_value > 1:
            current_value -= 1
        self.zoom_scale.set(current_value)
        self.update_zoom()

    def on_press1(self, event):
        self.start_x1 = event.x
        self.start_y1 = event.y

    def on_drag1(self, event):
        if self.start_x1 and self.start_y1:
            self.x_offset1 = event.x - self.start_x1
            self.y_offset1 = event.y - self.start_y1
            self.current_x1 += self.x_offset1  # Update current position
            self.current_y1 += self.y_offset1  # Update current position
            self.canvas.move("video", self.x_offset1, self.y_offset1)
            self.start_x1 = event.x
            self.start_y1 = event.y
```

```python
    def on_press2(self, event):
        self.start_x2 = event.x
        self.start_y2 = event.y

    def on_drag2(self, event):
        if self.start_x2 and self.start_y2:
            self.x_offset2 = event.x - self.start_x2
            self.y_offset2 = event.y - self.start_y2
            self.current_x2 += self.x_offset2  # Update current position
            self.current_y2 += self.y_offset2  # Update current position
            self.flow_canvas.move("mask", self.x_offset2, self.y_offset2)  # Move optical flow canvas along with original canvas
            self.start_x2 = event.x
            self.start_y2 = event.y

    def jump_to_time(self):
        time_str = self.time_entry.get()
        try:
            time_seconds = float(time_str)
            if 0 <= time_seconds:
                self.frame_index = int(time_seconds * self.video.get_meta_data()['fps'])
                self.show_frame()
                self.show_optical_flow()  # Jump to specified time for optical flow
        except ValueError:
            pass

    def prev_frame(self):
        if self.frame_index > 0:
            self.frame_index -= 1
            self.show_frame()
            self.show_optical_flow()
            print(self.frame_index)

    def next_frame(self):
        if self.video and self.frame_index < len(self.video) - 1:
            self.show_frame()
            self.show_optical_flow()
            print(self.frame_index)

    def set_window_title(self):
        if self.file_name:
            self.master.title(f"Motion Estimation with Gradient-Based Block Matching Algorithm (GBBM) and Lucas-Kanade - {self.file_name}")
            self.master.title_font = ("Helvetica", 16, "bold")
        else:
```

```python
        self.master.title("Motion Estimation with Gradient-Based Block Matching Algorithm (GBBM) and Lucas-Kanade")

    def open_another_player(self):
        # Open another instance of the application
        root = tk.Toplevel(self.master)
        app = VideoGBBM_LK_OpticalFlow(root)

def main():
    root = tk.Tk()
    app = VideoGBBM_LK_OpticalFlow(root)
    root.mainloop()

if __name__ == "__main__":
    main()
```

COMBINING MOTION ESTIMATION WITH GRADIENT-BASED BLOCK MATCHING ALGORITHM (GBBM) AND SIFT

DESCRIPTION

This Python script, gui_motion_analysis_gbbm_sift.py, implements a graphical user interface (GUI) application for analyzing optical flow in videos using two different methods: the Gradient-Based Block Matching Algorithm (GBBM) and Scale-Invariant Feature Transform (SIFT). Let's break down the functionality and structure of the project.

The script begins by importing necessary libraries such as tkinter for GUI, PIL for image processing, imageio for video reading, and OpenCV for computer vision tasks like optical flow computation.

The VideoGBBM_SIFT_OpticalFlow class serves as the main component of the application. It initializes the GUI window with various widgets such as buttons, comboboxes, and entry fields for user interaction.

Methods like create_widgets, open_video, play_video, show_frame, and show_optical_flow handle different aspects of the application, including video loading, playing, frame display, and optical flow computation and visualization.

The gradient_based_block_matching method implements the GBBM algorithm for computing optical flow, while the sift_optical_flow method utilizes the SIFT feature extraction algorithm to estimate motion vectors.

The GUI allows users to open video files, play/pause videos, stop videos, navigate frames, adjust zoom scale, and specify parameters such as step size, block size, search range, and motion vector scale.

Event handling functions like on_mousewheel, on_press1, on_drag1, on_press2, and on_drag2 manage user interactions such as zooming, panning, and dragging for both video display and optical flow visualization canvases.

The jump_to_time method enables users to jump to a specific time in the video, while the prev_frame and next_frame methods allow frame-by-frame navigation.

The set_window_title method updates the window title with the currently loaded video file name.

The open_another_player method creates another instance of the application for parallel video analysis.

The main function initializes the GUI application and starts the event loop.

Overall, this script provides a user-friendly interface for analyzing optical flow in videos using two different algorithms, offering insights into motion patterns and dynamics within the video content.

IMPLEMENTING SCALE-INVARIANT FEATURE TRANSFORM (SIFT) MOTION ESTIMATION

```python
    def sift_optical_flow(self, prev_frame_gray, frame_gray):
        sift = cv2.xfeatures2d.SIFT_create()
        keypoints_prev, descriptors_prev = sift.detectAndCompute(prev_frame_gray, None)
        keypoints_frame, descriptors_frame = sift.detectAndCompute(frame_gray, None)

        # Create BFMatcher object
        bf = cv2.BFMatcher()

        # Match descriptors
        matches = bf.knnMatch(descriptors_prev, descriptors_frame, k=2)

        # Apply ratio test
        good_matches = []
        for m, n in matches:
            if m.distance < 0.75 * n.distance:
                good_matches.append(m)

        # Estimate motion vectors from good matches
        motion_vectors = np.zeros((len(good_matches), 2))
        for i, match in enumerate(good_matches):
            # Get the keypoints for the matched points
            prev_point = keypoints_prev[match.queryIdx].pt
            frame_point = keypoints_frame[match.trainIdx].pt

            # Calculate the motion vector
            dx = frame_point[0] - prev_point[0]
            dy = frame_point[1] - prev_point[1]

            # Store the motion vector
            motion_vectors[i] = [dx, dy]

        return motion_vectors
```

This sift_optical_flow() function computes optical flow using the Scale-Invariant Feature Transform (SIFT) algorithm. Let's break down the steps:

1. SIFT Initialization: The function first creates an instance of the SIFT detector using cv2.xfeatures2d.SIFT_create().
2. Key Point Detection and Description: SIFT detects keypoints and computes descriptors for both the previous and current frames using the detectAndCompute

method. This step extracts distinctive features from the frames, allowing for robust matching.
3. Feature Matching: A Brute-Force Matcher (BFMatcher) object is created to match descriptors between the previous and current frames. knnMatch is used to find the k nearest neighbors for each descriptor.
4. Ratio Test: Matches are filtered using a ratio test to ensure that only high-quality matches are retained. For each match, if the distance to the closest neighbor is less than 75% of the distance to the second-closest neighbor, the match is considered good and retained.
5. Motion Vector Estimation: For each good match, the function calculates the motion vector by subtracting the coordinates of the matched keypoints between the previous and current frames. These motion vectors represent the displacement of keypoints between frames.
6. Storing Motion Vectors: The computed motion vectors are stored in a NumPy array, where each row corresponds to a motion vector with two components: dx (change in x-coordinate) and dy (change in y-coordinate).
7. Return: Finally, the function returns the array of motion vectors.

This function provides a robust method for estimating optical flow based on keypoint matching using the SIFT algorithm, which is particularly effective in scenarios with significant changes in viewpoint, illumination, and scale.

SHOWING OPTICAL FLOW

```
    def show_optical_flow(self):
        if self.video:
            if not self.paused:
                if 0 <= self.frame_index < len(self.video):  # Check if frame index is within range
                    try:
                        frame = self.video.get_data(self.frame_index)
                        frame_gray = cv2.cvtColor(frame, cv2.COLOR_RGB2GRAY)  # Convert to grayscale

                        # Calculate optical flow using Gradient-Based Block Matching Algorithm (GBBM)
                        motion_vectors_gbbm = self.gradient_based_block_matching(self.prev_frame_gray, frame_gray)

                        # Calculate optical flow using SIFT
```

```python
                        motion_vectors_sift = 
self.sift_optical_flow(self.prev_frame_gray, frame_gray)

                        # Create an empty mask image for visualization
                        mask = np.zeros_like(frame)

                        # Compute flow visualization for GBBM
                        step = int(self.step_entry.get())
                        for y in range(0, frame.shape[0], step):
                            for x in range(0, frame.shape[1], step):
                                # Ensure the motion vectors index does not exceed the 
bounds
                                if y // step < motion_vectors_gbbm.shape[0] and x // 
step < motion_vectors_gbbm.shape[1]:
                                    dx, dy = motion_vectors_gbbm[y // step, x // 
step]
                                    # Scale the optical flow vectors based on the 
zoom scale
                                    dx *= int(self.dx_entry.get())
                                    dy *= int(self.dx_entry.get())
                                    # Convert coordinates to integers
                                    x1, y1 = int(x), int(y)
                                    x2, y2 = int(x + dx), int(y + dy)
                                    # Draw the line and circle
                                    cv2.line(mask, (x1, y1), (x2, y2), (255, 255, 
255), 1)
                                    cv2.circle(mask, (x2, y2), 1, (0, 255, 0), -1)

                        # Compute flow visualization for SIFT
                        for dx, dy in motion_vectors_sift:
                            # Scale the optical flow vectors based on the zoom scale
                            dx *= int(self.dx_entry.get())
                            dy *= int(self.dx_entry.get())
                            # Draw the line and circle
                            x1, y1 = int(x), int(y)
                            x2, y2 = int(x + dx), int(y + dy)
                            cv2.line(mask, (x1, y1), (x2, y2), (255, 255, 255), 1)
                            cv2.circle(mask, (x2, y2), 1, (0, 255, 0), -1)

                        # Convert mask to PIL format and display on canvas
                        mask = Image.fromarray(mask)
                        mask = ImageTk.PhotoImage(mask)
                        self.mask = mask
                        self.flow_canvas.delete("mask")  # Delete previous optical 
flow
                        self.flow_canvas.create_image(self.current_x2, 
self.current_y2, anchor="nw", image=mask, tags="mask")
```

```
                # Update previous frame
                self.prev_frame_gray = frame_gray.copy()

        except Exception as e:
            print("Error in show_optical_flow:", e)  # Print error message
```

This show_optical_flow method() is responsible for visualizing the optical flow computed using both the Gradient-Based Block Matching Algorithm (GBBM) and the SIFT (Scale-Invariant Feature Transform) method. Let's break down its functionality:

1. Check Video Availability and Playback State:
    - The method first verifies that a video is loaded (self.video) and that the playback is not paused. It also ensures that the frame index is within the valid range of frames in the video.
2. Retrieve Current Frame:
    - It retrieves the current frame from the video using self.video.get_data(self.frame_index).
    - The frame is converted to grayscale using cv2.cvtColor(frame, cv2.COLOR_RGB2GRAY) to simplify optical flow computation.
3. Compute Optical Flow:
    - Optical flow is calculated using both the GBBM (gradient_based_block_matching) and SIFT (sift_optical_flow) methods. Each method returns a set of motion vectors representing the displacement of pixels between the current and previous frames.
4. Flow Visualization:
   For GBBM:
    - The computed motion vectors are visualized by drawing lines and circles on an empty mask image (mask) using OpenCV drawing functions (cv2.line and cv2.circle).
    - The vectors are scaled based on the zoom scale (self.dx_entry.get()) and the step size (self.step_entry.get()).
   For SIFT:
    - Similarly, the motion vectors obtained from the SIFT method are visualized on the same mask image.
5. Display on Canvas:
    - The mask image with visualized optical flow is converted to a format compatible with Tkinter (ImageTk.PhotoImage) and displayed on the self.flow_canvas widget.

- The previous frame (self.prev_frame_gray) is updated with the current frame to prepare for the next iteration.
6. Error Handling:

    Any exceptions that occur during the process are caught, and an error message is printed for debugging purposes.

Overall, this method provides real-time visualization of optical flow computed using two different algorithms, enhancing the user's understanding of motion dynamics in the video.

RUNNING PROGRAM

Run program and click on Open Video button. Then, choose a video file then click on Next Frame button.

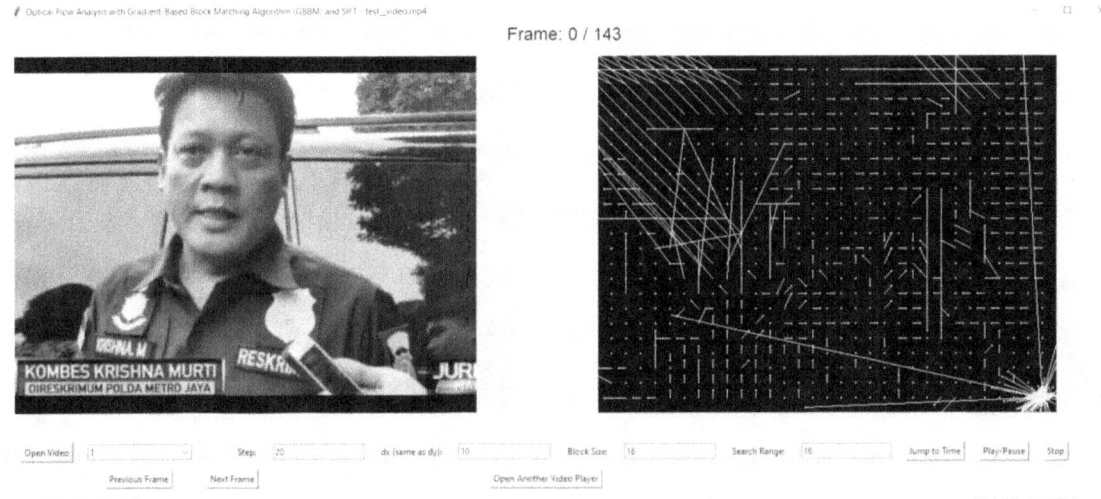

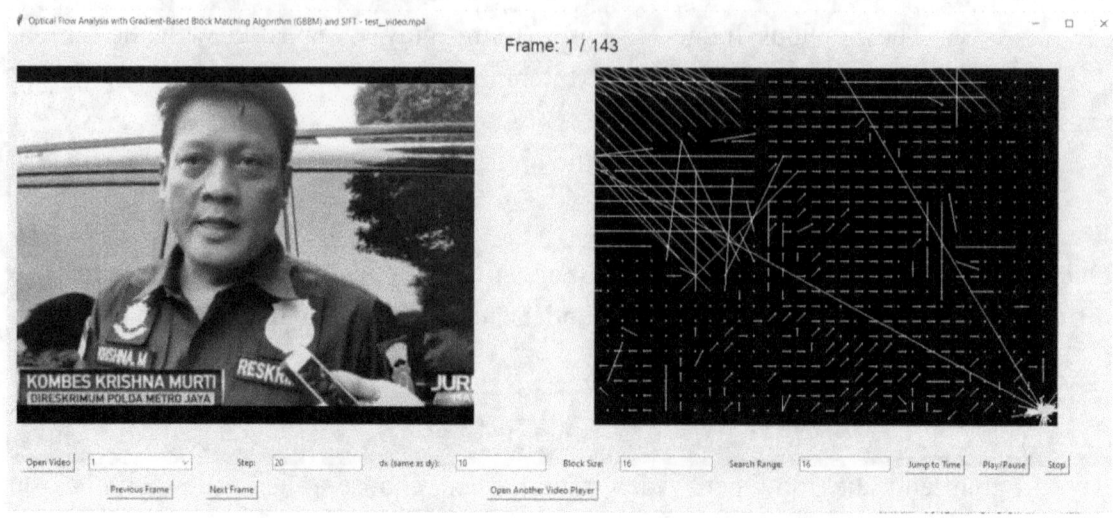

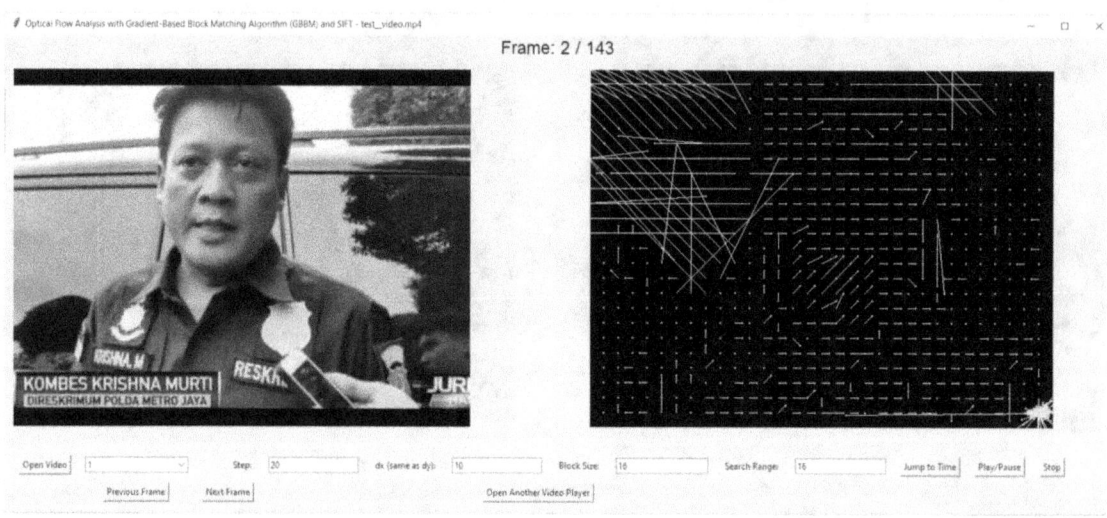

SOURCE CODE

```
#gui_motion_analysis_gbbm_sift.py
import tkinter as tk
from tkinter import ttk
from tkinter import filedialog
from PIL import Image, ImageTk
import imageio
import cv2
import numpy as np
```

```python
class VideoGBBM_SIFT_OpticalFlow:
    def __init__(self, master):
        self.master = master
        self.master.title("Optical Flow Analysis with Gradient-Based Block Matching Algorithm (GBBM) and SIFT")
        self.file_name = ""
        self.set_window_title()  # Set window title initially

        # Frame number label
        self.frame_number_label = tk.Label(master, text="Frame: 0")
        self.frame_number_label.pack()

        self.video = None
        self.video_path = None
        self.paused = False
        self.zoom_scale = tk.IntVar(value=1)
        self.frame_index = 0
        self.start_x1 = None
        self.start_y1 = None
        self.current_x1 = 0
        self.current_y1 = 0
        self.start_x2 = None
        self.start_y2 = None
        self.current_x2 = 0
        self.current_y2 = 0

        self.prev_frame_gray = None  # Initialize prev_frame_gray variable
        self.create_widgets()

    def create_widgets(self):
        # Panel for video display
        video_panel = tk.Frame(self.master)
        video_panel.pack(padx=10, pady=10)

        # Canvas to display the original video
        canvas_width = 800
        canvas_height = 500
        self.canvas = tk.Canvas(video_panel, width=canvas_width, height=canvas_height)
        self.canvas.pack(side="left", fill="both", expand=True)
        self.canvas.bind("<MouseWheel>", self.on_mousewheel)
        self.canvas.bind("<ButtonPress-1>", self.on_press1)
        self.canvas.bind("<B1-Motion>", self.on_drag1)

        # Canvas to display the optical flow result
        self.flow_canvas = tk.Canvas(video_panel, width=canvas_width, height=canvas_height)
```

```python
        self.flow_canvas.pack(side="right", fill="both", expand=True)
        self.flow_canvas.bind("<MouseWheel>", self.on_mousewheel)
        self.flow_canvas.bind("<ButtonPress-1>", self.on_press2)
        self.flow_canvas.bind("<B1-Motion>", self.on_drag2)

        # Panel for control buttons
        control_panel = tk.Frame(self.master)
        control_panel.pack(padx=10, pady=(0, 10), fill="x")

        # Button to open a video file
        self.open_button = tk.Button(control_panel, text="Open Video", command=self.open_video)
        self.open_button.grid(row=0, column=0, padx=10, pady=5)

        # Combobox for selecting zoom scale
        self.zoom_combobox = ttk.Combobox(control_panel, textvariable=self.zoom_scale, values=list(range(1, 11)))
        self.zoom_combobox.grid(row=0, column=1, padx=10, pady=5)
        self.zoom_combobox.bind("<<ComboboxSelected>>", self.update_zoom)

        # Label and entry for specifying step
        self.step_label = tk.Label(control_panel, text="Step:")
        self.step_label.grid(row=0, column=2, padx=10, pady=5, sticky="e")
        self.step_default = tk.StringVar(value="20")
        self.step_entry = ttk.Entry(control_panel, textvariable=self.step_default)
        self.step_entry.grid(row=0, column=3, padx=10, pady=5, sticky="w")
        self.step_entry.bind("<Return>", lambda event: self.toggle_play_pause())

        # Label and entry for specifying dx (same as dy)
        self.dx_label = tk.Label(control_panel, text="dx (same as dy):")
        self.dx_label.grid(row=0, column=4, padx=10, pady=5, sticky="e")
        self.dx_default = tk.StringVar(value="10")
        self.dx_entry = ttk.Entry(control_panel, textvariable=self.dx_default)
        self.dx_entry.grid(row=0, column=5, padx=10, pady=5, sticky="w")
        self.dx_entry.bind("<Return>", lambda event: self.toggle_play_pause())

        # Label and entry for specifying block size
        self.block_size_label = tk.Label(control_panel, text="Block Size:")
        self.block_size_label.grid(row=0, column=6, padx=10, pady=5, sticky="e")
        self.block_size_default = tk.StringVar(value="16")
        self.block_size_entry = ttk.Entry(control_panel, textvariable=self.block_size_default)
        self.block_size_entry.grid(row=0, column=7, padx=10, pady=5, sticky="w")
        self.block_size_entry.bind("<Return>", lambda event: self.toggle_play_pause())

        # Label and entry for specifying search range
        self.search_range_label = tk.Label(control_panel, text="Search Range:")
```

```
        self.search_range_label.grid(row=0, column=8, padx=10, pady=5, sticky="e")
        self.search_range_default = tk.StringVar(value="16")
        self.search_range_entry = ttk.Entry(control_panel, 
textvariable=self.search_range_default)
        self.search_range_entry.grid(row=0, column=9, padx=10, pady=5, sticky="w")
        self.search_range_entry.bind("<Return>", lambda event: 
self.toggle_play_pause())

        # Button to jump to specified time
        self.jump_button = tk.Button(control_panel, text="Jump to Time", 
command=self.jump_to_time)
        self.jump_button.grid(row=0, column=10, padx=10, pady=5)

        # Button to play/pause the video
        self.play_button = tk.Button(control_panel, text="Play/Pause", 
command=self.toggle_play_pause)
        self.play_button.grid(row=0, column=11, padx=10, pady=5)

        # Button to stop the video
        self.stop_button = tk.Button(control_panel, text="Stop", 
command=self.stop_video)
        self.stop_button.grid(row=0, column=12, padx=10, pady=5)

        # Button to navigate to the previous frame
        self.prev_frame_button = tk.Button(control_panel, text="Previous Frame", 
command=self.prev_frame)
        self.prev_frame_button.grid(row=2, column=1, padx=10, pady=5)

        # Button to navigate to the next frame
        self.next_frame_button = tk.Button(control_panel, text="Next Frame", 
command=self.next_frame)
        self.next_frame_button.grid(row=2, column=2, padx=10, pady=5)

        # Button to open another instance of the application
        self.open_another_button = tk.Button(control_panel, text="Open Another Video 
Player", command=self.open_another_player)
        self.open_another_button.grid(row=2, column=0, columnspan=15, padx=10, 
pady=5)

    def open_video(self):
        self.video_path = filedialog.askopenfilename(filetypes=[("Video files", 
"*.mp4;*.avi;*.mkv")])
        if self.video_path:
            self.video = imageio.get_reader(self.video_path)
            self.file_name = self.video_path.split('/')[-1]  # Extract file name
            self.set_window_title()  # Update window title with file name
            self.play_video()
```

```python
    def play_video(self):
        if self.video:
            self.paused = False
            self.show_frame()
            self.show_optical_flow()

    def stop_video(self):
        self.paused = True
        self.frame_index = 0
        self.current_x1 = 0
        self.current_y1 = 0  # Reset the current position
        self.show_frame()
        self.show_optical_flow()

    def toggle_play_pause(self):
        self.paused = not self.paused
        if not self.paused:
            self.play_video()

    def update_zoom(self, event=None):
        self.show_frame()
        self.show_optical_flow()

    def show_frame(self):
        if self.video:
            if not self.paused:
                if 0 <= self.frame_index < len(self.video):  # Check if frame index is within range
                    try:
                        frame = self.video.get_data(self.frame_index)
                        frame_gray = cv2.cvtColor(frame, cv2.COLOR_RGB2GRAY)  # Convert to grayscale

                        # Initialize prev_frame_gray on first frame
                        if self.prev_frame_gray is None:
                            self.prev_frame_gray = frame_gray.copy()

                        # Display current frame
                        frame = Image.fromarray(frame)
                        frame = frame.resize((frame.width * self.zoom_scale.get(), frame.height * self.zoom_scale.get()))
                        photo = ImageTk.PhotoImage(frame)
                        self.photo = photo  # Save object reference to PhotoImage globally
                        self.canvas.delete("video")  # Delete previous image
                        self.canvas.create_image(self.current_x1, self.current_y1, anchor="nw", image=photo, tags="video")
```

```python
                    # Update prev_frame_gray
                    self.prev_frame_gray = frame_gray.copy()

                    # Update frame number label
                    self.frame_number_label.config(text=f"Frame: {self.frame_index} / {self.video.count_frames()}", font=("Helvetica", 18))

                    self.frame_index += 1  # Move to the next frame

            except Exception as e:
                print("Error: ", e)

    def gradient_based_block_matching(self, prev_frame_gray, frame_gray):
        # GBBM implementation
        block_size = int(self.block_size_entry.get())  # Get block size from entry
        search_range = int(self.search_range_entry.get())  # Get search range from entry
        motion_vectors = np.zeros((frame_gray.shape[0] // block_size, frame_gray.shape[1] // block_size, 2))

        # Compute gradient of the previous frame
        grad_x_prev = cv2.Sobel(prev_frame_gray, cv2.CV_64F, 1, 0, ksize=3)
        grad_y_prev = cv2.Sobel(prev_frame_gray, cv2.CV_64F, 0, 1, ksize=3)

        for y in range(0, frame_gray.shape[0] - block_size, block_size):
            for x in range(0, frame_gray.shape[1] - block_size, block_size):
                min_cost = float('inf')
                best_dx = 0
                best_dy = 0
                for dy in range(-search_range, search_range + 1):
                    for dx in range(-search_range, search_range + 1):
                        # Ensure the search area is within frame boundaries
                        if 0 <= y + dy < frame_gray.shape[0] - block_size and 0 <= x + dx < frame_gray.shape[1] - block_size:
                            template = prev_frame_gray[y:y+block_size, x:x+block_size]
                            search_area = frame_gray[y+dy:y+dy+block_size, x+dx:x+dx+block_size]

                            # Compute gradient of the search area
                            grad_x_search = cv2.Sobel(search_area, cv2.CV_64F, 1, 0, ksize=3)
                            grad_y_search = cv2.Sobel(search_area, cv2.CV_64F, 0, 1, ksize=3)

                            # Compute sum of squared differences of gradients
```

```python
                        ssd_grad = np.sum((grad_x_prev[y:y+block_size, 
x:x+block_size] - grad_x_search)**2 + (grad_y_prev[y:y+block_size, x:x+block_size] - 
grad_y_search)**2)
                        if ssd_grad < min_cost:
                            min_cost = ssd_grad
                            best_dx = dx
                            best_dy = dy
                motion_vectors[y // block_size, x // block_size] = [best_dx, best_dy]

        return motion_vectors

    def sift_optical_flow(self, prev_frame_gray, frame_gray):
        sift = cv2.xfeatures2d.SIFT_create()
        keypoints_prev, descriptors_prev = sift.detectAndCompute(prev_frame_gray, 
None)
        keypoints_frame, descriptors_frame = sift.detectAndCompute(frame_gray, None)

        # Create BFMatcher object
        bf = cv2.BFMatcher()

        # Match descriptors
        matches = bf.knnMatch(descriptors_prev, descriptors_frame, k=2)

        # Apply ratio test
        good_matches = []
        for m, n in matches:
            if m.distance < 0.75 * n.distance:
                good_matches.append(m)

        # Estimate motion vectors from good matches
        motion_vectors = np.zeros((len(good_matches), 2))
        for i, match in enumerate(good_matches):
            # Get the keypoints for the matched points
            prev_point = keypoints_prev[match.queryIdx].pt
            frame_point = keypoints_frame[match.trainIdx].pt

            # Calculate the motion vector
            dx = frame_point[0] - prev_point[0]
            dy = frame_point[1] - prev_point[1]

            # Store the motion vector
            motion_vectors[i] = [dx, dy]

        return motion_vectors

    def show_optical_flow(self):
        if self.video:
            if not self.paused:
```

```python
            if 0 <= self.frame_index < len(self.video):  # Check if frame index is within range
                try:
                    frame = self.video.get_data(self.frame_index)
                    frame_gray = cv2.cvtColor(frame, cv2.COLOR_RGB2GRAY)  # Convert to grayscale

                    # Calculate optical flow using Gradient-Based Block Matching Algorithm (GBBM)
                    motion_vectors_gbbm = self.gradient_based_block_matching(self.prev_frame_gray, frame_gray)

                    # Calculate optical flow using SIFT
                    motion_vectors_sift = self.sift_optical_flow(self.prev_frame_gray, frame_gray)

                    # Create an empty mask image for visualization
                    mask = np.zeros_like(frame)

                    # Compute flow visualization for GBBM
                    step = int(self.step_entry.get())
                    for y in range(0, frame.shape[0], step):
                        for x in range(0, frame.shape[1], step):
                            # Ensure the motion vectors index does not exceed the bounds
                            if y // step < motion_vectors_gbbm.shape[0] and x // step < motion_vectors_gbbm.shape[1]:
                                dx, dy = motion_vectors_gbbm[y // step, x // step]
                                # Scale the optical flow vectors based on the zoom scale
                                dx *= int(self.dx_entry.get())
                                dy *= int(self.dx_entry.get())
                                # Convert coordinates to integers
                                x1, y1 = int(x), int(y)
                                x2, y2 = int(x + dx), int(y + dy)
                                # Draw the line and circle
                                cv2.line(mask, (x1, y1), (x2, y2), (255, 255, 255), 1)
                                cv2.circle(mask, (x2, y2), 1, (0, 255, 0), -1)

                    # Compute flow visualization for SIFT
                    for dx, dy in motion_vectors_sift:
                        # Scale the optical flow vectors based on the zoom scale
                        dx *= int(self.dx_entry.get())
                        dy *= int(self.dx_entry.get())
                        # Draw the line and circle
                        x1, y1 = int(x), int(y)
```

```python
                        x2, y2 = int(x + dx), int(y + dy)
                        cv2.line(mask, (x1, y1), (x2, y2), (255, 255, 255), 1)
                        cv2.circle(mask, (x2, y2), 1, (0, 255, 0), -1)

                    # Convert mask to PIL format and display on canvas
                    mask = Image.fromarray(mask)
                    mask = ImageTk.PhotoImage(mask)
                    self.mask = mask
                    self.flow_canvas.delete("mask")  # Delete previous optical flow
                    self.flow_canvas.create_image(self.current_x2, self.current_y2, anchor="nw", image=mask, tags="mask")

                    # Update previous frame
                    self.prev_frame_gray = frame_gray.copy()

        except Exception as e:
            print("Error in show_optical_flow:", e)  # Print error message

    def on_mousewheel(self, event):
        direction = event.delta // 120
        current_value = int(self.zoom_scale.get())
        if direction == 1 and current_value < 10:
            current_value += 1
        elif direction == -1 and current_value > 1:
            current_value -= 1
        self.zoom_scale.set(current_value)
        self.update_zoom()

    def on_press1(self, event):
        self.start_x1 = event.x
        self.start_y1 = event.y

    def on_drag1(self, event):
        if self.start_x1 and self.start_y1:
            self.x_offset1 = event.x - self.start_x1
            self.y_offset1 = event.y - self.start_y1
            self.current_x1 += self.x_offset1  # Update current position
            self.current_y1 += self.y_offset1  # Update current position
            self.canvas.move("video", self.x_offset1, self.y_offset1)
            self.start_x1 = event.x
            self.start_y1 = event.y

    def on_press2(self, event):
        self.start_x2 = event.x
        self.start_y2 = event.y
```

```python
    def on_drag2(self, event):
        if self.start_x2 and self.start_y2:
            self.x_offset2 = event.x - self.start_x2
            self.y_offset2 = event.y - self.start_y2
            self.current_x2 += self.x_offset2  # Update current position
            self.current_y2 += self.y_offset2  # Update current position
            self.flow_canvas.move("mask", self.x_offset2, self.y_offset2)  # Move
optical flow canvas along with original canvas
            self.start_x2 = event.x
            self.start_y2 = event.y

    def jump_to_time(self):
        time_str = self.time_entry.get()
        try:
            time_seconds = float(time_str)
            if 0 <= time_seconds:
                self.frame_index = int(time_seconds *
self.video.get_meta_data()['fps'])
                self.show_frame()
                self.show_optical_flow()  # Jump to specified time for optical flow
        except ValueError:
            pass

    def prev_frame(self):
        if self.frame_index > 0:
            self.frame_index -= 1
            self.show_frame()
            self.show_optical_flow()
            print(self.frame_index)

    def next_frame(self):
        if self.video and self.frame_index < len(self.video) - 1:
            self.show_frame()
            self.show_optical_flow()
            print(self.frame_index)

    def set_window_title(self):
        if self.file_name:
            self.master.title(f"Optical Flow Analysis with Gradient-Based Block
Matching Algorithm (GBBM) and SIFT - {self.file_name}")
            self.master.title_font = ("Helvetica", 16, "bold")
        else:
            self.master.title("Optical Flow Analysis with Gradient-Based Block
Matching Algorithm (GBBM) and SIFT")

    def open_another_player(self):
        # Open another instance of the application
        root = tk.Toplevel(self.master)
```

```python
        app = VideoGBBM_SIFT_OpticalFlow(root)

def main():
    root = tk.Tk()
    app = VideoGBBM_SIFT_OpticalFlow(root)
    root.mainloop()

if __name__ == "__main__":
    main()
```

COMBINING MOTION ESTIMATION WITH GRADIENT-BASED BLOCK MATCHING ALGORITHM (GBBM) AND ORB

DESCRIPTION

This project, implemented in the gui_motion_analysis_gbbm_orb.py script, serves the purpose of providing a user-friendly interface for motion estimation in videos using two different techniques: the Gradient-Based Block Matching Algorithm (GBBM) and ORB (Oriented FAST and Rotated BRIEF) optical flow. The primary aim is to enable users to analyze and visualize the motion dynamics within a video file.

The GUI application offers various functionalities to facilitate the analysis process. Users can open video files of common formats (e.g., MP4, AVI, MKV) through a file dialog. Once a video is loaded, the application displays the frames on a canvas, allowing users to navigate through the frames using control buttons like play, pause, stop, next frame, and previous frame.

Additionally, the application provides options to adjust the zoom scale, step size, and other parameters relevant to motion estimation algorithms. Users can fine-tune these parameters to optimize the analysis based on the characteristics of the video content and the specific requirements of their analysis.

The core functionality of the application lies in computing and visualizing the optical flow using both the GBBM and ORB algorithms. Optical flow, which represents the apparent motion of objects in a video, is visualized using vectors overlaid on the video frames. This visualization helps users understand how objects move across consecutive frames, revealing important motion patterns and dynamics.

Furthermore, the application supports interactive features such as mouse wheel zooming and dragging to navigate and explore the video frames and optical flow visualizations more conveniently. Users can dynamically adjust the viewing perspective to focus on specific regions of interest or analyze motion at different scales.

Overall, the project aims to provide a comprehensive tool for motion analysis in videos, offering both intuitive user interface elements and advanced motion estimation techniques. By combining ease of use with powerful analysis capabilities, the application empowers users to gain insights into motion behavior and patterns within video data for various applications, including surveillance, sports analysis, and computer vision research.

IMPLEMENTING ORB (ORIENTED FAST AND ROTATED BRIEF)

ORB (Oriented FAST and Rotated BRIEF) is a feature detection and description algorithm used in computer vision for tasks such as object recognition, image registration, and optical flow estimation. It was developed to address the limitations of existing feature detection methods like SIFT (Scale-Invariant Feature Transform) and SURF (Speeded-Up Robust Features) in terms of computational efficiency and robustness.

Here's a breakdown of its key components and how it works:
1. FAST (Features from Accelerated Segment Test):
    - FAST is a corner detection algorithm that identifies interest points (keypoints) in an image based on pixel intensity variations.

- It operates by comparing the intensity of a central pixel to the intensities of pixels in a circle around it.
- If a sufficient number of contiguous pixels are brighter or darker than the central pixel, it is classified as a corner.
- FAST is computationally efficient, making it suitable for real-time applications.

2. BRIEF (Binary Robust Independent Elementary Features):

- BRIEF is a feature descriptor that encodes local image information into a binary string.
- It operates by comparing pixel intensities at predetermined pairs of points within a patch surrounding a keypoint.
- The resulting binary string represents a unique feature descriptor for the keypoint.
- BRIEF descriptors are lightweight and fast to compute, but they lack robustness to changes in scale, rotation, and lighting conditions.

3. Orientation Assignment:
   - ORB introduces orientation assignment to make the descriptors rotationally invariant.
   - After identifying keypoints using FAST, ORB computes a dominant orientation for each keypoint based on gradient information.
   - The orientation is determined by analyzing the distribution of gradients in the patch around the keypoint.
   - Descriptors are then computed relative to this orientation, enabling robustness to image rotations.

4. Rotation Invariance:
   - By incorporating orientation information into the feature descriptors, ORB achieves rotation invariance.
   - This means that even if an object in the scene is rotated, the corresponding feature descriptors will remain consistent and matchable.

5. Matching:
   - ORB descriptors are binary strings, which allows for efficient matching using techniques like Hamming distance.
   - Matching involves finding correspondences between keypoints in different images by comparing their binary descriptors.

- Keypoints with similar descriptors are considered potential matches, and further filtering (e.g., based on distance ratios) is often applied to improve accuracy.

Overall, ORB offers a balance between computational efficiency and robustness, making it suitable for various computer vision applications, particularly those requiring real-time performance on resource-constrained devices. Its combination of FAST for keypoint detection, BRIEF for feature description, and orientation assignment for rotation invariance makes it a versatile and widely used algorithm in the field of computer vision.

```python
def orb_optical_flow(self, prev_frame_gray, frame_gray):
    orb = cv2.ORB_create()
    keypoints_prev, descriptors_prev = orb.detectAndCompute(prev_frame_gray, None)
    keypoints_frame, descriptors_frame = orb.detectAndCompute(frame_gray, None)

    # Create BFMatcher object
    bf = cv2.BFMatcher(cv2.NORM_HAMMING, crossCheck=True)

    # Match descriptors
    matches = bf.match(descriptors_prev, descriptors_frame)

    # Estimate motion vectors from matches
    motion_vectors = np.zeros((len(matches), 2))
    for i, match in enumerate(matches):
        # Get the keypoints for the matched points
        prev_point = keypoints_prev[match.queryIdx].pt
        frame_point = keypoints_frame[match.trainIdx].pt

        # Calculate the motion vector
        dx = frame_point[0] - prev_point[0]
        dy = frame_point[1] - prev_point[1]

        # Store the motion vector
        motion_vectors[i] = [dx, dy]

    return motion_vectors
```

This orb_optical_flow() function computes optical flow using the ORB (Oriented FAST and Rotated BRIEF) feature detection and description algorithm. Here's a breakdown of how it works:
1. ORB Initialization:

The function initializes an ORB object using cv2.ORB_create(). This object is used to detect keypoints and compute descriptors for each frame.
2. KeyPoint Detection and Description:
    - It then detects keypoints and computes descriptors for both the previous and current frames using the ORB object.
    - orb.detectAndCompute(prev_frame_gray, None) and orb.detectAndCompute(frame_gray, None) detect keypoints and compute descriptors for the previous and current frames, respectively.
    - prev_frame_gray and frame_gray are the grayscale versions of the previous and current frames.
3. Feature Matching:
    - After obtaining the descriptors for both frames, a Brute-Force Matcher (BFMatcher) object is created using cv2.BFMatcher(cv2.NORM_HAMMING, crossCheck=True). This matcher is specifically tailored for binary descriptors like those produced by ORB.
    - The match method of the BFMatcher is then used to find matches between descriptors of corresponding keypoints in the previous and current frames.
4. Motion Vector Estimation:
    - For each matched pair of keypoints, the function calculates the motion vector by subtracting the coordinates of the corresponding keypoints between the two frames.
    - The motion vector (dx, dy) represents the horizontal and vertical displacements of the keypoints from the previous frame to the current frame.
    - These motion vectors are stored in a numpy array motion_vectors.
5. Return:
    - Finally, the function returns the array of motion vectors computed from the matches between keypoints in the previous and current frames.

Overall, this function leverages the ORB algorithm to detect and describe keypoints in consecutive frames and computes optical flow by estimating motion vectors between corresponding keypoints. This approach provides a simple yet effective method for tracking motion between frames in a video sequence.

SHOWING OPTICAL FLOW

```python
    def show_optical_flow(self):
        if self.video:
            if not self.paused:
                if 0 <= self.frame_index < len(self.video):  # Check if frame index is within range
                    try:
                        frame = self.video.get_data(self.frame_index)
                        frame_gray = cv2.cvtColor(frame, cv2.COLOR_RGB2GRAY)  # Convert to grayscale

                        # Calculate optical flow using Gradient-Based Block Matching Algorithm (GBBM)
                        motion_vectors_gbbm = self.gradient_based_block_matching(self.prev_frame_gray, frame_gray)

                        # Calculate optical flow using ORB
                        motion_vectors_orb = self.orb_optical_flow(self.prev_frame_gray, frame_gray)

                        # Create an empty mask image for visualization
                        mask = np.zeros_like(frame)

                        # Compute flow visualization for GBBM
                        step = int(self.step_entry.get())
                        for y in range(0, frame.shape[0], step):
                            for x in range(0, frame.shape[1], step):
                                # Ensure the motion vectors index does not exceed the bounds
                                if y // step < motion_vectors_gbbm.shape[0] and x // step < motion_vectors_gbbm.shape[1]:
                                    dx, dy = motion_vectors_gbbm[y // step, x // step]
                                    # Scale the optical flow vectors based on the zoom scale
                                    dx *= int(self.dx_entry.get())
                                    dy *= int(self.dx_entry.get())
                                    # Convert coordinates to integers
                                    x1, y1 = int(x), int(y)
                                    x2, y2 = int(x + dx), int(y + dy)
                                    # Draw the line and circle
                                    cv2.line(mask, (x1, y1), (x2, y2), (255, 255, 255), 1)
                                    cv2.circle(mask, (x2, y2), 1, (0, 255, 0), -1)

                        # Compute flow visualization for ORB
```

```
                    for dx, dy in motion_vectors_orb:
                        # Scale the optical flow vectors based on the zoom scale
                        dx *= int(self.dx_entry.get())
                        dy *= int(self.dx_entry.get())
                        # Draw the line and circle
                        x1, y1 = int(x), int(y)
                        x2, y2 = int(x + dx), int(y + dy)
                        cv2.line(mask, (x1, y1), (x2, y2), (255, 255, 255), 1)
                        cv2.circle(mask, (x2, y2), 1, (0, 255, 0), -1)

                    # Convert mask to PIL format and display on canvas
                    mask = Image.fromarray(mask)
                    mask = ImageTk.PhotoImage(mask)
                    self.mask = mask
                    self.flow_canvas.delete("mask")  # Delete previous optical
flow
                    self.flow_canvas.create_image(self.current_x2,
self.current_y2, anchor="nw", image=mask, tags="mask")

                    # Update previous frame
                    self.prev_frame_gray = frame_gray.copy()

            except Exception as e:
                print("Error in show_optical_flow:", e)  # Print error
message
```

The show_optical_flow() method is a crucial part of the class responsible for displaying the computed optical flow on a canvas. Let's dissect its functionality:

1. Check Video and Paused Status:

   The method first checks if a video is loaded (self.video) and if it's not paused. This ensures that the method is only executed when there's a video being played and it's not paused.

2. Frame Index Check:

   It verifies whether the current frame index (self.frame_index) is within the range of the loaded video frames.

3. Frame Retrieval and Grayscale Conversion:
   - It retrieves the current frame from the video using self.video.get_data(self.frame_index).
   - The frame is then converted to grayscale using cv2.cvtColor(frame, cv2.COLOR_RGB2GRAY). This conversion simplifies further processing for optical flow computation.

4. Optical Flow Calculation:

- Optical flow is calculated using two different methods: Gradient-Based Block Matching Algorithm (GBBM) and ORB (Oriented FAST and Rotated BRIEF).
- motion_vectors_gbbm and motion_vectors_orb store the motion vectors computed using GBBM and ORB, respectively.

5. Flow Visualization:
    - The computed motion vectors are used to generate a visual representation of the optical flow.
    - For GBBM, it iterates over the motion vectors and draws lines and circles on the mask image to represent the flow.
    - Similarly, for ORB, it iterates over the motion vectors and adds flow visualization to the mask image.

6. Display on Canvas:
    - The mask image, containing the flow visualization, is converted to a format compatible with Tkinter's canvas.
    - The previous optical flow on the canvas is deleted (self.flow_canvas.delete("mask")), and the new flow visualization is created at the appropriate position on the canvas.

7. Update Previous Frame:
    Finally, the prev_frame_gray is updated with the current frame's grayscale version for subsequent optical flow computation in the next frame.

8. Error Handling:
    Exception handling is implemented to catch and print any errors that might occur during the execution of the method.

Overall, this method encapsulates the process of computing and displaying optical flow in the video player application, allowing users to visualize the motion between consecutive frames using both GBBM and ORB algorithms.

RUNNING PROGRAM

Run program and click on Open Video button. Then, choose a video file then click on Next Frame button.

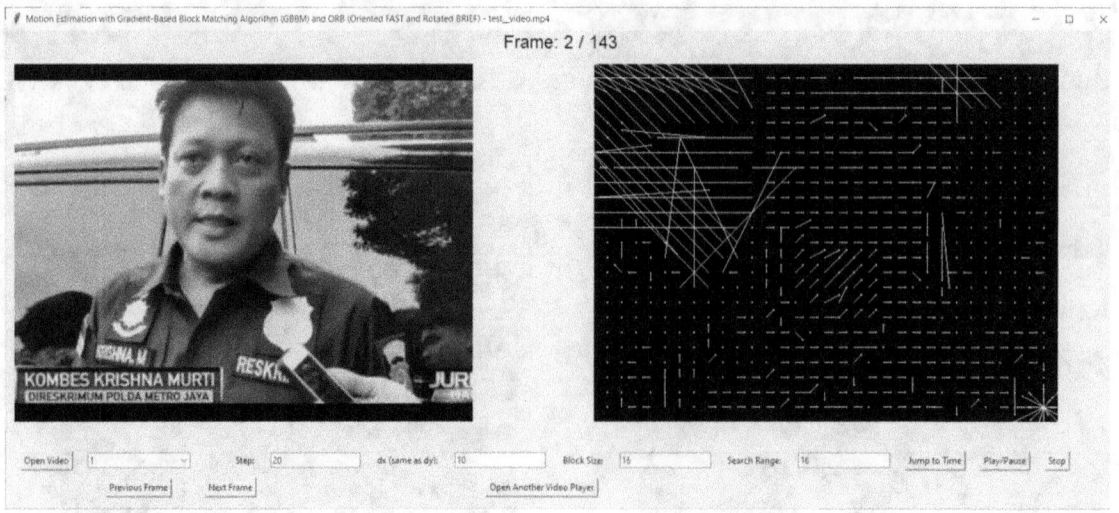

SOURCE CODE

```python
#gui_motion_analysis_gbbm_orb.py
import tkinter as tk
from tkinter import ttk
from tkinter import filedialog
from PIL import Image, ImageTk
import imageio
import cv2
import numpy as np

class VideoGBBM_ORB_OpticalFlow:
    def __init__(self, master):
        self.master = master
        self.master.title("Motion Estimation with Gradient-Based Block Matching Algorithm (GBBM) and ORB (Oriented FAST and Rotated BRIEF)")
        self.file_name = ""
        self.set_window_title()  # Set window title initially

        # Frame number label
        self.frame_number_label = tk.Label(master, text="Frame: 0")
        self.frame_number_label.pack()

        self.video = None
        self.video_path = None
        self.paused = False
        self.zoom_scale = tk.IntVar(value=1)
        self.frame_index = 0
        self.start_x1 = None
```

```python
        self.start_y1 = None
        self.current_x1 = 0
        self.current_y1 = 0
        self.start_x2 = None
        self.start_y2 = None
        self.current_x2 = 0
        self.current_y2 = 0

        self.prev_frame_gray = None  # Initialize prev_frame_gray variable
        self.create_widgets()

    def create_widgets(self):
        # Panel for video display
        video_panel = tk.Frame(self.master)
        video_panel.pack(padx=10, pady=10)

        # Canvas to display the original video
        canvas_width = 800
        canvas_height = 500
        self.canvas = tk.Canvas(video_panel, width=canvas_width, height=canvas_height)
        self.canvas.pack(side="left", fill="both", expand=True)
        self.canvas.bind("<MouseWheel>", self.on_mousewheel)
        self.canvas.bind("<ButtonPress-1>", self.on_press1)
        self.canvas.bind("<B1-Motion>", self.on_drag1)

        # Canvas to display the optical flow result
        self.flow_canvas = tk.Canvas(video_panel, width=canvas_width, height=canvas_height)
        self.flow_canvas.pack(side="right", fill="both", expand=True)
        self.flow_canvas.bind("<MouseWheel>", self.on_mousewheel)
        self.flow_canvas.bind("<ButtonPress-1>", self.on_press2)
        self.flow_canvas.bind("<B1-Motion>", self.on_drag2)

        # Panel for control buttons
        control_panel = tk.Frame(self.master)
        control_panel.pack(padx=10, pady=(0, 10), fill="x")

        # Button to open a video file
        self.open_button = tk.Button(control_panel, text="Open Video", command=self.open_video)
        self.open_button.grid(row=0, column=0, padx=10, pady=5)

        # Combobox for selecting zoom scale
        self.zoom_combobox = ttk.Combobox(control_panel, textvariable=self.zoom_scale, values=list(range(1, 11)))
        self.zoom_combobox.grid(row=0, column=1, padx=10, pady=5)
        self.zoom_combobox.bind("<<ComboboxSelected>>", self.update_zoom)
```

```python
        # Label and entry for specifying step
        self.step_label = tk.Label(control_panel, text="Step:")
        self.step_label.grid(row=0, column=2, padx=10, pady=5, sticky="e")
        self.step_default = tk.StringVar(value="20")
        self.step_entry = ttk.Entry(control_panel, textvariable=self.step_default)
        self.step_entry.grid(row=0, column=3, padx=10, pady=5, sticky="w")
        self.step_entry.bind("<Return>", lambda event: self.toggle_play_pause())

        # Label and entry for specifying dx (same as dy)
        self.dx_label = tk.Label(control_panel, text="dx (same as dy):")
        self.dx_label.grid(row=0, column=4, padx=10, pady=5, sticky="e")
        self.dx_default = tk.StringVar(value="10")
        self.dx_entry = ttk.Entry(control_panel, textvariable=self.dx_default)
        self.dx_entry.grid(row=0, column=5, padx=10, pady=5, sticky="w")
        self.dx_entry.bind("<Return>", lambda event: self.toggle_play_pause())

        # Label and entry for specifying block size
        self.block_size_label = tk.Label(control_panel, text="Block Size:")
        self.block_size_label.grid(row=0, column=6, padx=10, pady=5, sticky="e")
        self.block_size_default = tk.StringVar(value="16")
        self.block_size_entry = ttk.Entry(control_panel, textvariable=self.block_size_default)
        self.block_size_entry.grid(row=0, column=7, padx=10, pady=5, sticky="w")
        self.block_size_entry.bind("<Return>", lambda event: self.toggle_play_pause())

        # Label and entry for specifying search range
        self.search_range_label = tk.Label(control_panel, text="Search Range:")
        self.search_range_label.grid(row=0, column=8, padx=10, pady=5, sticky="e")
        self.search_range_default = tk.StringVar(value="16")
        self.search_range_entry = ttk.Entry(control_panel, textvariable=self.search_range_default)
        self.search_range_entry.grid(row=0, column=9, padx=10, pady=5, sticky="w")
        self.search_range_entry.bind("<Return>", lambda event: self.toggle_play_pause())

        # Button to jump to specified time
        self.jump_button = tk.Button(control_panel, text="Jump to Time", command=self.jump_to_time)
        self.jump_button.grid(row=0, column=10, padx=10, pady=5)

        # Button to play/pause the video
        self.play_button = tk.Button(control_panel, text="Play/Pause", command=self.toggle_play_pause)
        self.play_button.grid(row=0, column=11, padx=10, pady=5)

        # Button to stop the video
```

```python
        self.stop_button = tk.Button(control_panel, text="Stop", command=self.stop_video)
        self.stop_button.grid(row=0, column=12, padx=10, pady=5)

        # Button to navigate to the previous frame
        self.prev_frame_button = tk.Button(control_panel, text="Previous Frame", command=self.prev_frame)
        self.prev_frame_button.grid(row=2, column=1, padx=10, pady=5)

        # Button to navigate to the next frame
        self.next_frame_button = tk.Button(control_panel, text="Next Frame", command=self.next_frame)
        self.next_frame_button.grid(row=2, column=2, padx=10, pady=5)

        # Button to open another instance of the application
        self.open_another_button = tk.Button(control_panel, text="Open Another Video Player", command=self.open_another_player)
        self.open_another_button.grid(row=2, column=0, columnspan=15, padx=10, pady=5)

    def open_video(self):
        self.video_path = filedialog.askopenfilename(filetypes=[("Video files", "*.mp4;*.avi;*.mkv")])
        if self.video_path:
            self.video = imageio.get_reader(self.video_path)
            self.file_name = self.video_path.split('/')[-1]  # Extract file name
            self.set_window_title()  # Update window title with file name
            self.play_video()

    def play_video(self):
        if self.video:
            self.paused = False
            self.show_frame()
            self.show_optical_flow()

    def stop_video(self):
        self.paused = True
        self.frame_index = 0
        self.current_x1 = 0
        self.current_y1 = 0  # Reset the current position
        self.show_frame()
        self.show_optical_flow()

    def toggle_play_pause(self):
        self.paused = not self.paused
        if not self.paused:
            self.play_video()
```

```python
    def update_zoom(self, event=None):
        self.show_frame()
        self.show_optical_flow()

    def show_frame(self):
        if self.video:
            if not self.paused:
                if 0 <= self.frame_index < len(self.video):  # Check if frame index is within range
                    try:
                        frame = self.video.get_data(self.frame_index)
                        frame_gray = cv2.cvtColor(frame, cv2.COLOR_RGB2GRAY)  # Convert to grayscale

                        # Initialize prev_frame_gray on first frame
                        if self.prev_frame_gray is None:
                            self.prev_frame_gray = frame_gray.copy()

                        # Display current frame
                        frame = Image.fromarray(frame)
                        frame = frame.resize((frame.width * self.zoom_scale.get(), frame.height * self.zoom_scale.get()))
                        photo = ImageTk.PhotoImage(frame)
                        self.photo = photo  # Save object reference to PhotoImage globally
                        self.canvas.delete("video")  # Delete previous image
                        self.canvas.create_image(self.current_x1, self.current_y1, anchor="nw", image=photo, tags="video")

                        # Update prev_frame_gray
                        self.prev_frame_gray = frame_gray.copy()

                        # Update frame number label
                        self.frame_number_label.config(text=f"Frame: {self.frame_index} / {self.video.count_frames()}", font=("Helvetica", 18))

                        self.frame_index += 1  # Move to the next frame

                    except Exception as e:
                        print("Error: ", e)

    def gradient_based_block_matching(self, prev_frame_gray, frame_gray):
        # GBBM implementation
        block_size = int(self.block_size_entry.get())  # Get block size from entry
        search_range = int(self.search_range_entry.get())  # Get search range from entry
        motion_vectors = np.zeros((frame_gray.shape[0] // block_size, frame_gray.shape[1] // block_size, 2))
```

```python
            # Compute gradient of the previous frame
            grad_x_prev = cv2.Sobel(prev_frame_gray, cv2.CV_64F, 1, 0, ksize=3)
            grad_y_prev = cv2.Sobel(prev_frame_gray, cv2.CV_64F, 0, 1, ksize=3)

            for y in range(0, frame_gray.shape[0] - block_size, block_size):
                for x in range(0, frame_gray.shape[1] - block_size, block_size):
                    min_cost = float('inf')
                    best_dx = 0
                    best_dy = 0
                    for dy in range(-search_range, search_range + 1):
                        for dx in range(-search_range, search_range + 1):
                            # Ensure the search area is within frame boundaries
                            if 0 <= y + dy < frame_gray.shape[0] - block_size and 0 <= x + dx < frame_gray.shape[1] - block_size:
                                template = prev_frame_gray[y:y+block_size, x:x+block_size]
                                search_area = frame_gray[y+dy:y+dy+block_size, x+dx:x+dx+block_size]

                                # Compute gradient of the search area
                                grad_x_search = cv2.Sobel(search_area, cv2.CV_64F, 1, 0, ksize=3)
                                grad_y_search = cv2.Sobel(search_area, cv2.CV_64F, 0, 1, ksize=3)

                                # Compute sum of squared differences of gradients
                                ssd_grad = np.sum((grad_x_prev[y:y+block_size, x:x+block_size] - grad_x_search)**2 + (grad_y_prev[y:y+block_size, x:x+block_size] - grad_y_search)**2)
                                if ssd_grad < min_cost:
                                    min_cost = ssd_grad
                                    best_dx = dx
                                    best_dy = dy
                    motion_vectors[y // block_size, x // block_size] = [best_dx, best_dy]

        return motion_vectors

    def orb_optical_flow(self, prev_frame_gray, frame_gray):
        orb = cv2.ORB_create()
        keypoints_prev, descriptors_prev = orb.detectAndCompute(prev_frame_gray, None)
        keypoints_frame, descriptors_frame = orb.detectAndCompute(frame_gray, None)

        # Create BFMatcher object
        bf = cv2.BFMatcher(cv2.NORM_HAMMING, crossCheck=True)

        # Match descriptors
```

```python
            matches = bf.match(descriptors_prev, descriptors_frame)

            # Estimate motion vectors from matches
            motion_vectors = np.zeros((len(matches), 2))
            for i, match in enumerate(matches):
                # Get the keypoints for the matched points
                prev_point = keypoints_prev[match.queryIdx].pt
                frame_point = keypoints_frame[match.trainIdx].pt

                # Calculate the motion vector
                dx = frame_point[0] - prev_point[0]
                dy = frame_point[1] - prev_point[1]

                # Store the motion vector
                motion_vectors[i] = [dx, dy]

            return motion_vectors

    def show_optical_flow(self):
        if self.video:
            if not self.paused:
                if 0 <= self.frame_index < len(self.video):  # Check if frame index is within range
                    try:
                        frame = self.video.get_data(self.frame_index)
                        frame_gray = cv2.cvtColor(frame, cv2.COLOR_RGB2GRAY)  # Convert to grayscale

                        # Calculate optical flow using Gradient-Based Block Matching Algorithm (GBBM)
                        motion_vectors_gbbm = self.gradient_based_block_matching(self.prev_frame_gray, frame_gray)

                        # Calculate optical flow using ORB
                        motion_vectors_orb = self.orb_optical_flow(self.prev_frame_gray, frame_gray)

                        # Create an empty mask image for visualization
                        mask = np.zeros_like(frame)

                        # Compute flow visualization for GBBM
                        step = int(self.step_entry.get())
                        for y in range(0, frame.shape[0], step):
                            for x in range(0, frame.shape[1], step):
                                # Ensure the motion vectors index does not exceed the bounds
                                if y // step < motion_vectors_gbbm.shape[0] and x // step < motion_vectors_gbbm.shape[1]:
```

```python
                                    dx, dy = motion_vectors_gbbm[y // step, x // step]
                                    # Scale the optical flow vectors based on the zoom scale
                                    dx *= int(self.dx_entry.get())
                                    dy *= int(self.dx_entry.get())
                                    # Convert coordinates to integers
                                    x1, y1 = int(x), int(y)
                                    x2, y2 = int(x + dx), int(y + dy)
                                    # Draw the line and circle
                                    cv2.line(mask, (x1, y1), (x2, y2), (255, 255, 255), 1)
                                    cv2.circle(mask, (x2, y2), 1, (0, 255, 0), -1)

                            # Compute flow visualization for ORB
                            for dx, dy in motion_vectors_orb:
                                # Scale the optical flow vectors based on the zoom scale
                                dx *= int(self.dx_entry.get())
                                dy *= int(self.dx_entry.get())
                                # Draw the line and circle
                                x1, y1 = int(x), int(y)
                                x2, y2 = int(x + dx), int(y + dy)
                                cv2.line(mask, (x1, y1), (x2, y2), (255, 255, 255), 1)
                                cv2.circle(mask, (x2, y2), 1, (0, 255, 0), -1)

                            # Convert mask to PIL format and display on canvas
                            mask = Image.fromarray(mask)
                            mask = ImageTk.PhotoImage(mask)
                            self.mask = mask
                            self.flow_canvas.delete("mask")  # Delete previous optical flow
                            self.flow_canvas.create_image(self.current_x2, self.current_y2, anchor="nw", image=mask, tags="mask")

                            # Update previous frame
                            self.prev_frame_gray = frame_gray.copy()

                    except Exception as e:
                        print("Error in show_optical_flow:", e)  # Print error message

    def on_mousewheel(self, event):
        direction = event.delta // 120
        current_value = int(self.zoom_scale.get())
        if direction == 1 and current_value < 10:
            current_value += 1
        elif direction == -1 and current_value > 1:
            current_value -= 1
```

```python
            self.zoom_scale.set(current_value)
            self.update_zoom()

    def on_press1(self, event):
        self.start_x1 = event.x
        self.start_y1 = event.y

    def on_drag1(self, event):
        if self.start_x1 and self.start_y1:
            self.x_offset1 = event.x - self.start_x1
            self.y_offset1 = event.y - self.start_y1
            self.current_x1 += self.x_offset1  # Update current position
            self.current_y1 += self.y_offset1  # Update current position
            self.canvas.move("video", self.x_offset1, self.y_offset1)
            self.start_x1 = event.x
            self.start_y1 = event.y

    def on_press2(self, event):
        self.start_x2 = event.x
        self.start_y2 = event.y

    def on_drag2(self, event):
        if self.start_x2 and self.start_y2:
            self.x_offset2 = event.x - self.start_x2
            self.y_offset2 = event.y - self.start_y2
            self.current_x2 += self.x_offset2  # Update current position
            self.current_y2 += self.y_offset2  # Update current position
            self.flow_canvas.move("mask", self.x_offset2, self.y_offset2)  # Move
optical flow canvas along with original canvas
            self.start_x2 = event.x
            self.start_y2 = event.y

    def jump_to_time(self):
        time_str = self.time_entry.get()
        try:
            time_seconds = float(time_str)
            if 0 <= time_seconds:
                self.frame_index = int(time_seconds *
self.video.get_meta_data()['fps'])
                self.show_frame()
                self.show_optical_flow()  # Jump to specified time for optical flow
        except ValueError:
            pass

    def prev_frame(self):
        if self.frame_index > 0:
            self.frame_index -= 1
            self.show_frame()
```

```python
            self.show_optical_flow()
            print(self.frame_index)

    def next_frame(self):
        if self.video and self.frame_index < len(self.video) - 1:
            self.show_frame()
            self.show_optical_flow()
            print(self.frame_index)

    def set_window_title(self):
        if self.file_name:
            self.master.title(f"Motion Estimation with Gradient-Based Block Matching Algorithm (GBBM) and ORB (Oriented FAST and Rotated BRIEF) - {self.file_name}")
            self.master.title_font = ("Helvetica", 16, "bold")
        else:
            self.master.title("Motion Estimation with Gradient-Based Block Matching Algorithm (GBBM) and ORB (Oriented FAST and Rotated BRIEF)")

    def open_another_player(self):
        # Open another instance of the application
        root = tk.Toplevel(self.master)
        app = VideoGBBM_ORB_OpticalFlow(root)

def main():
    root = tk.Tk()
    app = VideoGBBM_ORB_OpticalFlow(root)
    root.mainloop()

if __name__ == "__main__":
    main()
```

OBJECT TRACKING WITH GRADIENT-BASED BLOCK MATCHING ALGORITHM (GBBM)

DESCRIPTION

The project is an implementation of object tracking using the Gradient-Based Block Matching Algorithm (GBBM). Object tracking plays a crucial role in various computer vision applications such as surveillance, robotics, and human-computer interaction. By continuously locating and following objects of interest in a video stream, this project aims to demonstrate the practical application of GBBM for real-time object tracking.

The graphical user interface (GUI) of the application allows users to interact with video files easily. Users can open video files in common formats like MP4, AVI, MKV, and WMV using the provided "Open Video" button. Once a video is loaded, it is displayed on the canvas, enabling users to visualize the frames.

The application provides controls for playing, pausing, and stopping the video playback. Users can navigate through the video frames using the "Previous Frame" and "Next Frame" buttons. Additionally, a combobox allows users to adjust the zoom scale for better visualization of the video frames.

The heart of the project lies in the implementation of the Gradient-Based Block Matching Algorithm (GBBM) for object tracking. GBBM estimates the motion of an object between consecutive frames by comparing blocks of pixels. The algorithm iterates through each block in the current frame and searches for the most similar block in the previous frame within a specified search range. By computing the displacement of each block, GBBM generates motion vectors that describe the object's motion.

During object tracking, users can select a region of interest (ROI) on the video frame by clicking and dragging the mouse. The application tracks the movement of the selected object within the ROI using GBBM. The object's trajectory is displayed in real-time, showing the calculated center coordinates of the object on the listbox.

The GUI also provides options for adjusting parameters such as block size and search range, allowing users to fine-tune the performance of the object tracking algorithm according to their specific requirements. These parameters significantly impact the accuracy and computational efficiency of the tracking process.

Furthermore, the application offers visual feedback by displaying the bounding box around the tracked object on the video canvas. This bounding box dynamically adjusts its position based on the estimated motion of the object, providing users with a visual representation of the object's movement throughout the video.

Overall, the project serves as an educational tool for understanding and experimenting with object tracking techniques, specifically focusing on the Gradient-Based Block Matching Algorithm. It demonstrates how computer vision algorithms can be applied to track objects in videos and offers a practical example of implementing such algorithms within a user-friendly interface.

CREATING WIDGETS

```python
def create_widgets(self):
    # Panel for video display
    video_panel = tk.Frame(self.master)
    video_panel.pack(padx=10, pady=10)

    # Canvas to display the original video
```

```python
        canvas_width = 800
        canvas_height = 500
        self.canvas = tk.Canvas(video_panel, width=canvas_width, 
height=canvas_height)
        self.canvas.pack(side="left", fill="both", expand=True)
        self.canvas.bind("<MouseWheel>", self.on_mousewheel)
        self.canvas.bind("<ButtonPress-1>", self.on_press)
        self.canvas.bind("<B1-Motion>", self.on_drag)
        
        # List box to display center coordinates
        self.center_listbox = tk.Listbox(video_panel, width=30, height=20, 
font=("Helvetica", 14))
        self.center_listbox.pack(side="right", fill="y")
        # Scrollbar for the listbox
        scrollbar = tk.Scrollbar(video_panel, orient="vertical")
        scrollbar.pack(side="left", fill="y")
        scrollbar.config(command=self.center_listbox.yview)

        # Attach scrollbar to listbox
        self.center_listbox.config(yscrollcommand=scrollbar.set)
        
        # Panel for control buttons
        control_panel = tk.Frame(self.master)
        control_panel.pack(padx=10, pady=(0, 10), fill="x")

        # Button to open a video file
        self.open_button = tk.Button(control_panel, text="Open Video", 
command=self.open_video)
        self.open_button.grid(row=0, column=0, padx=10, pady=5)

        # Combobox for selecting zoom scale
        self.zoom_combobox = ttk.Combobox(control_panel, 
textvariable=self.zoom_scale, values=list(range(1, 11)))
        self.zoom_combobox.grid(row=0, column=1, padx=10, pady=5)
        self.zoom_combobox.bind("<<ComboboxSelected>>", self.update_zoom)

        # Button to play/pause the video
        self.play_button = tk.Button(control_panel, text="Play/Pause", 
command=self.toggle_play_pause)
        self.play_button.grid(row=0, column=2, padx=10, pady=5)

        # Button to stop the video
        self.stop_button = tk.Button(control_panel, text="Stop", 
command=self.stop_video)
        self.stop_button.grid(row=0, column=3, padx=10, pady=5)

        # Button to navigate to the previous frame
```

```python
        self.prev_frame_button = tk.Button(control_panel, text="Previous Frame",
command=self.prev_frame)
        self.prev_frame_button.grid(row=0, column=4, padx=10, pady=5)

        # Button to navigate to the next frame
        self.next_frame_button = tk.Button(control_panel, text="Next Frame",
command=self.next_frame)
        self.next_frame_button.grid(row=0, column=5, padx=10, pady=5)

        # Button to clear the listbox
        self.clear_button = tk.Button(control_panel, text="Clear Listbox",
command=self.clear_listbox)
        self.clear_button.grid(row=0, column=6, padx=10, pady=5)

        # Label and entry for specifying block size
        self.block_size_label = tk.Label(control_panel, text="Block Size:")
        self.block_size_label.grid(row=0, column=7, padx=10, pady=5, sticky="e")
        self.block_size_default = tk.StringVar(value="16")
        self.block_size_entry = ttk.Entry(control_panel,
textvariable=self.block_size_default)
        self.block_size_entry.grid(row=0, column=8, padx=10, pady=5, sticky="w")
        self.block_size_entry.bind("<Return>", lambda event:
self.toggle_play_pause())

        # Label and entry for specifying search range
        self.search_range_label = tk.Label(control_panel, text="Search Range:")
        self.search_range_label.grid(row=0, column=9, padx=10, pady=5, sticky="e")
        self.search_range_default = tk.StringVar(value="16")
        self.search_range_entry = ttk.Entry(control_panel,
textvariable=self.search_range_default)
        self.search_range_entry.grid(row=0, column=10, padx=10, pady=5, sticky="w")
        self.search_range_entry.bind("<Return>", lambda event:
self.toggle_play_pause())
```

The create_widgets() method is responsible for setting up the graphical user interface (GUI) elements of the application. Let's break down each part:

1. Video Panel and Canvas: This section creates a frame (video_panel) to hold the video canvas. The canvas (self.canvas) is where the video frames will be displayed. It's configured to have a fixed width and height, and it binds mouse events such as scrolling, mouse press, and mouse drag to corresponding event handler methods.
2. Center Listbox: Another frame (video_panel) is created to hold a listbox (self.center_listbox). This listbox will display the center coordinates of the tracked

object. A vertical scrollbar is attached to the listbox to enable scrolling through the coordinates.
3. Control Panel: This section creates a frame (control_panel) to hold control buttons for video playback and other functionalities.
4. Open Video Button: Clicking this button (self.open_button) triggers the open_video method, allowing users to select and load a video file.
5. Zoom Combobox: Users can select the zoom scale using this combobox (self.zoom_combobox). Changes in the zoom scale trigger the update_zoom method.
6. Play/Pause Button: This button (self.play_button) toggles between playing and pausing the video when clicked. Its functionality is handled by the toggle_play_pause method.
7. Stop Button: Clicking this button (self.stop_button) stops the video playback and resets the frame index to 0.
8. Previous Frame Button: Clicking this button (self.prev_frame_button) navigates to the previous frame in the video sequence.
9. Next Frame Button: Clicking this button (self.next_frame_button) navigates to the next frame in the video sequence.
10. Clear Listbox Button: Clicking this button (self.clear_button) clears the content of the center coordinates listbox.
11. Block Size Entry: Users can specify the block size for the Gradient-Based Block Matching Algorithm using this entry field (self.block_size_entry). Pressing Enter in this entry field triggers the toggle_play_pause method.
12. Search Range Entry: Similar to the block size entry, users can specify the search range for the algorithm using this entry field (self.search_range_entry). Pressing Enter triggers the toggle_play_pause method.

Overall, this method sets up the necessary GUI elements and their associated functionalities for the object tracking application.

TRACKING OBJECT

```python
def gradient_based_block_matching(self, prev_frame_gray, frame_gray):
    # GBBM implementation
    block_size = int(self.block_size_entry.get())  # Get block size from entry
    search_range = int(self.search_range_entry.get())  # Get search range from entry
```

```python
            motion_vectors = np.zeros((frame_gray.shape[0] // block_size, 
frame_gray.shape[1] // block_size, 2))

            for y in range(0, frame_gray.shape[0] - block_size, block_size):
                for x in range(0, frame_gray.shape[1] - block_size, block_size):
                    min_cost = float('inf')
                    best_dx = 0
                    best_dy = 0
                    for dy in range(-search_range, search_range + 1):
                        for dx in range(-search_range, search_range + 1):
                            # Ensure the search area is within frame boundaries
                            if 0 <= y + dy < frame_gray.shape[0] - block_size and 0 <= x 
+ dx < frame_gray.shape[1] - block_size:
                                template = prev_frame_gray[y:y + block_size, x:x + 
block_size]
                                search_area = frame_gray[y + dy:y + dy + block_size, x + 
dx:x + dx + block_size]
                                
                                # Compute sum of squared differences
                                ssd = np.sum((template - search_area) ** 2)
                                
                                if ssd < min_cost:
                                    min_cost = ssd
                                    best_dx = dx
                                    best_dy = dy
                    motion_vectors[y // block_size, x // block_size] = [best_dx, best_dy]

        return motion_vectors

    def track_object(self, frame, bbox):
        if bbox:
            x1, y1, x2, y2 = map(int, bbox)
            roi = frame[y1:y2, x1:x2]
            if roi.size > 0:
                # Convert the ROI to grayscale
                roi_gray = cv2.cvtColor(roi, cv2.COLOR_BGR2GRAY)
                # Initialize the previous frame if not already initialized or if its 
dimensions don't match the current frame
                if self.prev_frame_gray is None or self.prev_frame_gray.shape != 
roi_gray.shape:
                    self.prev_frame_gray = roi_gray.copy()

                # Calculate motion vectors using gradient-based block matching
                motion_vectors = 
self.gradient_based_block_matching(self.prev_frame_gray, roi_gray)

                # Calculate the mean motion vector within the bounding box
                mean_motion_vector = np.mean(motion_vectors, axis=(0, 1))
```

```python
            # Update the bounding box coordinates based on the mean motion vector
            x1 += int(mean_motion_vector[0])
            y1 += int(mean_motion_vector[1])
            x2 += int(mean_motion_vector[0])
            y2 += int(mean_motion_vector[1])

            # Update the previous frame
            self.prev_frame_gray = roi_gray.copy()

            # Calculate the center of the bounding box
            center_x = (x1 + x2) // 2
            center_y = (y1 + y2) // 2

            # Add the center coordinates to the list box
            self.center_listbox.insert(tk.END, f"(center_x = {center_x}, center_y = {center_y})")

            return x1, y1, x2, y2
    return None
```

The gradient_based_block_matching() method implements the Gradient-Based Block Matching (GBBM) algorithm, while the track_object() method utilizes this algorithm for object tracking. Let's dissect each method:

gradient_based_block_matching() method:
1. This method takes two grayscale frames, prev_frame_gray (previous frame) and frame_gray (current frame), as input.
2. It starts by extracting the block size and search range from the GUI elements block_size_entry and search_range_entry.
3. It initializes an array motion_vectors to store the motion vectors for each block.
4. Then, it iterates over each block in the current frame using nested loops.
5. Within each block, it performs a search in a local neighborhood defined by the search range to find the best match with the corresponding block in the previous frame.
6. The best match is determined by minimizing the sum of squared differences (SSD) between the template block from the previous frame and the search area in the current frame.
7. The motion vector with the lowest SSD is stored in the motion_vectors array.
8. Finally, it returns the array of motion vectors.

track_object() method:
1. This method tracks the object within the specified bounding box (bbox) in the current frame (frame).
2. It first extracts the region of interest (ROI) from the frame based on the bounding box coordinates.
3. If the ROI is not empty, it converts it to grayscale and initializes the previous frame (prev_frame_gray) if necessary.
4. It then calculates the motion vectors using the gradient_based_block_matching method.
5. The mean motion vector within the bounding box is computed.
6. The bounding box coordinates are updated based on this mean motion vector to estimate the object's new position.
7. The center coordinates of the updated bounding box are added to the center listbox for display.
8. Finally, the updated bounding box coordinates are returned.

These methods work together to implement object tracking using the Gradient-Based Block Matching Algorithm, where the motion between consecutive frames is estimated by comparing blocks of pixels. The mean motion vector within the bounding box provides an estimate of the object's movement, enabling real-time tracking within a video sequence.

UPDATING BOUNDING BOX RECTANGLE

```
def update_bbox_rectangle(self, bbox):
    if bbox is not None:
        x1, y1, x2, y2 = map(int, bbox)
        if self.bbox_rect is not None:
            self.canvas.coords(self.bbox_rect, x1, y1, x2, y2)
            self.canvas.tag_raise(self.bbox_rect)  # Raise the bounding box to the front
        else:
            self.bbox_rect = self.canvas.create_rectangle(x1, y1, x2-50, y2-50, outline='#fc3d3d', width=8, tags="bbox")
```

The update_bbox_rectangle() method is responsible for updating the visualization of the bounding box rectangle on the canvas. Let's break down its functionality:
1. It takes the bounding box coordinates (bbox) as input.

2. If the bounding box is not None, it proceeds to update the rectangle visualization on the canvas.
3. It extracts the coordinates of the bounding box (x1, y1, x2, y2) using map and converts them to integers.
4. If the bbox_rect attribute is not None, it means that a bounding box rectangle has already been created on the canvas. In this case, it updates the coordinates of the existing rectangle using the coords method of the canvas.
5. Additionally, it raises the bounding box rectangle to the front using the tag_raise method to ensure it's visible above other canvas elements.
6. If bbox_rect is None, it means that there's no existing bounding box rectangle on the canvas. In this case, it creates a new rectangle using the create_rectangle method of the canvas. The rectangle's dimensions are defined by x1, y1, x2, y2, with an outline color of #fc3d3d, a width of 8, and it's tagged with "bbox".

By updating or creating the bounding box rectangle visualization, this method ensures that the tracked object's position is visually represented on the canvas for the user to see.

SHOWING TRACKED OBJECT

```python
def show_frame(self):
    if self.video:
        if not self.paused:
            if 0 <= self.frame_index < len(self.video):
                if not self.frame_processing:  # Check if the frame is already being processed
                    try:
                        self.frame_processing = True  # Set frame_processing flag to True to indicate frame processing

                        frame = self.video.get_data(self.frame_index)
                        frame = cv2.cvtColor(frame, cv2.COLOR_RGB2BGR)

                        if self.bbox is not None:
                            if not self.tracking_started:
                                self.tracking_started = True

                            self.bbox = self.track_object(frame, self.bbox)
                            if self.bbox:
                                frame = cv2.cvtColor(frame, cv2.COLOR_BGR2RGB)
                                frame = Image.fromarray(frame)
```

```
                                frame = frame.resize((frame.width *
self.zoom_scale.get(), frame.height * self.zoom_scale.get()))
                                photo = ImageTk.PhotoImage(frame)
                                self.photo = photo
                                self.canvas.delete("video")
                                self.canvas.create_image(0, 0, anchor="nw",
image=photo, tags="video")
                                self.update_bbox_rectangle(self.bbox)

                        else:
                            frame = cv2.cvtColor(frame, cv2.COLOR_BGR2RGB)
                            frame = Image.fromarray(frame)
                            frame = frame.resize((frame.width *
self.zoom_scale.get(), frame.height * self.zoom_scale.get()))
                            photo = ImageTk.PhotoImage(frame)
                            self.photo = photo
                            self.canvas.delete("video")
                            self.canvas.create_image(0, 0, anchor="nw",
image=photo, tags="video")

                        self.frame_number_label.config(text=f"Frame:
{self.frame_index} / {self.video.count_frames()}", font=("Helvetica", 18))

                        self.frame_index += 1

            except Exception as e:
                print("Error: ", e)
            finally:
                self.frame_processing = False    # Reset frame_processing
flag to False after processing the frame
```

The show_frame() method is central to displaying video frames on the canvas while handling object tracking and user interaction. Let's dissect its functionality:

1. It first checks if there is a video loaded (self.video is not None) and if the video is not paused (self.paused is False).
2. Next, it ensures that the current frame index (self.frame_index) is within the range of available frames in the video.
3. If the frame is not already being processed (self.frame_processing is False), it proceeds to process the frame.
4. Upon starting frame processing, it sets self.frame_processing to True to indicate that the frame is being processed.
5. It retrieves the current frame from the video using self.video.get_data(self.frame_index) and converts it from RGB to BGR format using OpenCV's cv2.cvtColor.

6. If object tracking is enabled (a bounding box self.bbox is defined), it tracks the object within the frame using the track_object method.
7. If the bounding box is successfully tracked (self.bbox is not None), it converts the frame back to RGB format, resizes it based on the zoom scale, creates an ImageTk.PhotoImage object from the resized frame, updates self.photo attribute, deletes the existing video display on the canvas ("video" tag), creates a new image item with the updated frame, and updates the bounding box rectangle visualization using update_bbox_rectangle.
8. If object tracking is not enabled (no bounding box defined), it simply converts the frame to RGB format, resizes it based on the zoom scale, creates an ImageTk.PhotoImage object, updates self.photo, deletes the existing video display on the canvas, and creates a new image item with the updated frame.
9. The method also updates the frame number label to display the current frame index and the total number of frames in the video.
10. Finally, it increments the frame index to process the next frame and sets self.frame_processing back to False to indicate that frame processing is complete.

Overall, show_frame() ensures the smooth display of video frames on the canvas, handling object tracking when enabled, and updating the user interface components accordingly.

RUNNING PROGRAM

Run program and click on Open Video button. Then, choose a video file then click on Next Frame button.

SOURCE CODE

```
# object_tracking_gbbm.py
import tkinter as tk
from tkinter import ttk
from tkinter import filedialog
from PIL import Image, ImageTk
import imageio
import cv2
import numpy as np

class ObjectTrackingGBBM:
    def __init__(self, master):
        self.master = master
        self.master.title("Object Tracking with Gradient-Based Block Matching Algorithm (GBBM)")
        self.file_name = ""
        self.set_window_title()  # Set window title initially

        self.frame_number_label = tk.Label(master, text="Frame: 0")
```

```python
        self.frame_number_label.pack()

        self.video = None
        self.video_path = None
        self.paused = False
        self.zoom_scale = tk.IntVar(value=1)
        self.frame_index = 0
        self.bbox = None
        self.tracking_started = False  # Initialize tracking_started to False
        self.prev_frame_gray = None

        self.bbox_rect = None  # Initialize bbox_rect attribute to None
        self.frame_processing = False  # Initialize frame_processing attribute to False

        self.create_widgets()

    def create_widgets(self):
        # Panel for video display
        video_panel = tk.Frame(self.master)
        video_panel.pack(padx=10, pady=10)

        # Canvas to display the original video
        canvas_width = 800
        canvas_height = 500
        self.canvas = tk.Canvas(video_panel, width=canvas_width, height=canvas_height)
        self.canvas.pack(side="left", fill="both", expand=True)
        self.canvas.bind("<MouseWheel>", self.on_mousewheel)
        self.canvas.bind("<ButtonPress-1>", self.on_press)
        self.canvas.bind("<B1-Motion>", self.on_drag)

        # List box to display center coordinates
        self.center_listbox = tk.Listbox(video_panel, width=30, height=20, font=("Helvetica", 14))
        self.center_listbox.pack(side="right", fill="y")
        # Scrollbar for the listbox
        scrollbar = tk.Scrollbar(video_panel, orient="vertical")
        scrollbar.pack(side="left", fill="y")
        scrollbar.config(command=self.center_listbox.yview)

        # Attach scrollbar to listbox
        self.center_listbox.config(yscrollcommand=scrollbar.set)

        # Panel for control buttons
        control_panel = tk.Frame(self.master)
        control_panel.pack(padx=10, pady=(0, 10), fill="x")
```

```python
        # Button to open a video file
        self.open_button = tk.Button(control_panel, text="Open Video", 
command=self.open_video)
        self.open_button.grid(row=0, column=0, padx=10, pady=5)

        # Combobox for selecting zoom scale
        self.zoom_combobox = ttk.Combobox(control_panel, 
textvariable=self.zoom_scale, values=list(range(1, 11)))
        self.zoom_combobox.grid(row=0, column=1, padx=10, pady=5)
        self.zoom_combobox.bind("<<ComboboxSelected>>", self.update_zoom)

        # Button to play/pause the video
        self.play_button = tk.Button(control_panel, text="Play/Pause", 
command=self.toggle_play_pause)
        self.play_button.grid(row=0, column=2, padx=10, pady=5)

        # Button to stop the video
        self.stop_button = tk.Button(control_panel, text="Stop", 
command=self.stop_video)
        self.stop_button.grid(row=0, column=3, padx=10, pady=5)

        # Button to navigate to the previous frame
        self.prev_frame_button = tk.Button(control_panel, text="Previous Frame", 
command=self.prev_frame)
        self.prev_frame_button.grid(row=0, column=4, padx=10, pady=5)

        # Button to navigate to the next frame
        self.next_frame_button = tk.Button(control_panel, text="Next Frame", 
command=self.next_frame)
        self.next_frame_button.grid(row=0, column=5, padx=10, pady=5)

        # Button to clear the listbox
        self.clear_button = tk.Button(control_panel, text="Clear Listbox", 
command=self.clear_listbox)
        self.clear_button.grid(row=0, column=6, padx=10, pady=5)

        # Label and entry for specifying block size
        self.block_size_label = tk.Label(control_panel, text="Block Size:")
        self.block_size_label.grid(row=0, column=7, padx=10, pady=5, sticky="e")
        self.block_size_default = tk.StringVar(value="16")
        self.block_size_entry = ttk.Entry(control_panel, 
textvariable=self.block_size_default)
        self.block_size_entry.grid(row=0, column=8, padx=10, pady=5, sticky="w")
        self.block_size_entry.bind("<Return>", lambda event: 
self.toggle_play_pause())

        # Label and entry for specifying search range
        self.search_range_label = tk.Label(control_panel, text="Search Range:")
```

```python
        self.search_range_label.grid(row=0, column=9, padx=10, pady=5, sticky="e")
        self.search_range_default = tk.StringVar(value="16")
        self.search_range_entry = ttk.Entry(control_panel, textvariable=self.search_range_default)
        self.search_range_entry.grid(row=0, column=10, padx=10, pady=5, sticky="w")
        self.search_range_entry.bind("<Return>", lambda event: self.toggle_play_pause())

    def open_video(self):
        self.video_path = filedialog.askopenfilename(filetypes=[("Video files", "*.mp4;*.avi;*.mkv;*.wmv")])
        if self.video_path:
            self.video = imageio.get_reader(self.video_path)
            self.file_name = self.video_path.split('/')[-1]
            self.set_window_title()
            self.play_video()

    def play_video(self):
        if self.video:
            self.paused = False
            self.tracking_started = True
            self.show_frame()

    def stop_video(self):
        self.paused = True
        self.frame_index = 0
        self.bbox = None
        self.show_frame()

    def toggle_play_pause(self):
        self.paused = not self.paused
        if not self.paused:
            if self.bbox is not None:
                self.tracking_started = True
            self.play_video()

    def update_zoom(self, event=None):
        self.show_frame()

    def gradient_based_block_matching(self, prev_frame_gray, frame_gray):
        # GBBM implementation
        block_size = int(self.block_size_entry.get())  # Get block size from entry
        search_range = int(self.search_range_entry.get())  # Get search range from entry
        motion_vectors = np.zeros((frame_gray.shape[0] // block_size, frame_gray.shape[1] // block_size, 2))

        for y in range(0, frame_gray.shape[0] - block_size, block_size):
```

```python
            for x in range(0, frame_gray.shape[1] - block_size, block_size):
                min_cost = float('inf')
                best_dx = 0
                best_dy = 0
                for dy in range(-search_range, search_range + 1):
                    for dx in range(-search_range, search_range + 1):
                        # Ensure the search area is within frame boundaries
                        if 0 <= y + dy < frame_gray.shape[0] - block_size and 0 <= x + dx < frame_gray.shape[1] - block_size:
                            template = prev_frame_gray[y:y + block_size, x:x + block_size]
                            search_area = frame_gray[y + dy:y + dy + block_size, x + dx:x + dx + block_size]

                            # Compute sum of squared differences
                            ssd = np.sum((template - search_area) ** 2)

                            if ssd < min_cost:
                                min_cost = ssd
                                best_dx = dx
                                best_dy = dy
                motion_vectors[y // block_size, x // block_size] = [best_dx, best_dy]

        return motion_vectors

    def track_object(self, frame, bbox):
        if bbox:
            x1, y1, x2, y2 = map(int, bbox)
            roi = frame[y1:y2, x1:x2]
            if roi.size > 0:
                # Convert the ROI to grayscale
                roi_gray = cv2.cvtColor(roi, cv2.COLOR_BGR2GRAY)
                # Initialize the previous frame if not already initialized or if its dimensions don't match the current frame
                if self.prev_frame_gray is None or self.prev_frame_gray.shape != roi_gray.shape:
                    self.prev_frame_gray = roi_gray.copy()

                # Calculate motion vectors using gradient-based block matching
                motion_vectors = self.gradient_based_block_matching(self.prev_frame_gray, roi_gray)

                # Calculate the mean motion vector within the bounding box
                mean_motion_vector = np.mean(motion_vectors, axis=(0, 1))

                # Update the bounding box coordinates based on the mean motion vector
                x1 += int(mean_motion_vector[0])
                y1 += int(mean_motion_vector[1])
```

```python
                x2 += int(mean_motion_vector[0])
                y2 += int(mean_motion_vector[1])

                # Update the previous frame
                self.prev_frame_gray = roi_gray.copy()

                # Calculate the center of the bounding box
                center_x = (x1 + x2) // 2
                center_y = (y1 + y2) // 2

                # Add the center coordinates to the list box
                self.center_listbox.insert(tk.END, f"(center_x = {center_x}, center_y = {center_y})")

                return x1, y1, x2, y2
        return None

    def update_bbox_rectangle(self, bbox):
        if bbox is not None:
            x1, y1, x2, y2 = map(int, bbox)
            if self.bbox_rect is not None:
                self.canvas.coords(self.bbox_rect, x1, y1, x2, y2)
                self.canvas.tag_raise(self.bbox_rect)  # Raise the bounding box to the front
            else:
                self.bbox_rect = self.canvas.create_rectangle(x1, y1, x2-50, y2-50, outline='#fc3d3d', width=8, tags="bbox")

    def show_frame(self):
        if self.video:
            if not self.paused:
                if 0 <= self.frame_index < len(self.video):
                    if not self.frame_processing:  # Check if the frame is already being processed
                        try:
                            self.frame_processing = True  # Set frame_processing flag to True to indicate frame processing

                            frame = self.video.get_data(self.frame_index)
                            frame = cv2.cvtColor(frame, cv2.COLOR_RGB2BGR)

                            if self.bbox is not None:
                                if not self.tracking_started:
                                    self.tracking_started = True

                                self.bbox = self.track_object(frame, self.bbox)
                                if self.bbox:
                                    frame = cv2.cvtColor(frame, cv2.COLOR_BGR2RGB)
```

```python
                                        frame = Image.fromarray(frame)
                                        frame = frame.resize((frame.width *
self.zoom_scale.get(), frame.height * self.zoom_scale.get()))
                                        photo = ImageTk.PhotoImage(frame)
                                        self.photo = photo
                                        self.canvas.delete("video")
                                        self.canvas.create_image(0, 0, anchor="nw",
image=photo, tags="video")
                                        self.update_bbox_rectangle(self.bbox)

                                else:
                                        frame = cv2.cvtColor(frame, cv2.COLOR_BGR2RGB)
                                        frame = Image.fromarray(frame)
                                        frame = frame.resize((frame.width *
self.zoom_scale.get(), frame.height * self.zoom_scale.get()))
                                        photo = ImageTk.PhotoImage(frame)
                                        self.photo = photo
                                        self.canvas.delete("video")
                                        self.canvas.create_image(0, 0, anchor="nw",
image=photo, tags="video")

                                self.frame_number_label.config(text=f"Frame:
{self.frame_index} / {self.video.count_frames()}", font=("Helvetica", 18))

                                self.frame_index += 1

                        except Exception as e:
                                print("Error: ", e)
                        finally:
                                self.frame_processing = False   # Reset frame_processing
flag to False after processing the frame

        def on_mousewheel(self, event):
                direction = event.delta // 120
                current_value = int(self.zoom_scale.get())
                if direction == 1 and current_value < 10:
                        current_value += 1
                elif direction == -1 and current_value > 1:
                        current_value -= 1
                self.zoom_scale.set(current_value)
                self.update_zoom()

        def on_press(self, event):
                self.start_x = self.canvas.canvasx(event.x)
                self.start_y = self.canvas.canvasy(event.y)
                self.bbox = None

        def on_drag(self, event):
```

```python
            cur_x = self.canvas.canvasx(event.x)
            cur_y = self.canvas.canvasy(event.y)
            if self.bbox_rect:
                self.canvas.delete(self.bbox_rect)
            self.bbox = (self.start_x, self.start_y, cur_x, cur_y)
            self.bbox_rect = self.canvas.create_rectangle(*self.bbox, outline='#fc3d3d', width=6)

    def prev_frame(self):
        if self.frame_index > 0:
            self.frame_index -= 1
            self.show_frame()

    def next_frame(self):
        if self.video and self.frame_index < len(self.video) - 1:
            self.show_frame()

    def clear_listbox(self):
        self.center_listbox.delete(0, tk.END)

    def set_window_title(self):
        if self.file_name:
            self.master.title(f"Object Tracking with Gradient-Based Block Matching Algorithm (GBBM) - {self.file_name}")
            self.master.title_font = ("Helvetica", 16, "bold")
        else:
            self.master.title("Object Tracking with Gradient-Based Block Matching Algorithm (GBBM)")

def main():
    root = tk.Tk()
    app = ObjectTrackingGBBM(root)
    root.mainloop()

if __name__ == "__main__":
    main()
```

OBJECT TRACKING WITH GRADIENT-BASED BLOCK MATCHING ALGORITHM (GBBM) WITH PYRAMID APPORACH

DESCRIPTION

This project aims to develop an application for object tracking using the Gradient-Based Block Matching Algorithm (GBBM) with a Pyramid Approach. Object tracking is a fundamental task in computer vision with numerous applications, such as surveillance, human-computer interaction, and autonomous vehicles.

The application provides a user-friendly interface built using the Tkinter library in Python. Upon launching the application, users are presented with a window containing controls and panels for video display, object tracking, and parameter adjustment.

Users can open video files of various formats (e.g., MP4, AVI) using the "Open Video" button, which initiates the object tracking process. Once a video is loaded, users can play, pause, stop, navigate through frames, and adjust zoom levels using intuitive control buttons and a combobox.

The heart of the application lies in the implementation of the GBBM algorithm with a pyramid approach for object tracking. This algorithm efficiently estimates motion vectors by iteratively refining the search space at multiple resolutions, enabling robust object tracking even in the presence of scale variations and occlusions.

The application visualizes the tracked object by drawing a bounding box around it on the video display canvas. Additionally, it dynamically updates a list box with the coordinates of the object's center, providing users with insights into the object's movement throughout the video.

Advanced features such as dynamic adjustment of block size and search range parameters further enhance the versatility and adaptability of the object tracking algorithm, allowing users to fine-tune the tracking process based on specific video characteristics and tracking requirements.

Overall, this project serves as a valuable tool for both novice and expert users in the field of computer vision, offering a practical implementation of a sophisticated object tracking algorithm within an accessible and customizable user interface.

TRACKING OBJECT

```python
def gradient_based_block_matching_pyramid(self, prev_frame_gray, frame_gray):
    # Initialize pyramid levels
    levels = int(self.level_entry.get())
    pyramid_prev = [prev_frame_gray]
    pyramid_frame = [frame_gray]
    for _ in range(levels - 1):
        prev_frame_gray = cv2.pyrDown(prev_frame_gray)
        frame_gray = cv2.pyrDown(frame_gray)
        pyramid_prev.append(prev_frame_gray)
        pyramid_frame.append(frame_gray)

    block_size = int(self.block_size_entry.get())  # Get block size from entry
    search_range = int(self.search_range_entry.get())  # Get search range from entry
```

```python
        motion_vectors = np.zeros((frame_gray.shape[0] // block_size, frame_gray.shape[1] // block_size, 2))

        for level in range(levels - 1, -1, -1):  # Iterate over pyramid levels in reverse order
            prev_frame_gray = pyramid_prev[level]
            frame_gray = pyramid_frame[level]
            block_size = block_size * (2 ** level)  # Adjust block size based on pyramid level
            search_range = search_range * (2 ** level)  # Adjust search range based on pyramid level

            # Compute gradient of the previous frame
            grad_x_prev = cv2.Sobel(prev_frame_gray, cv2.CV_64F, 1, 0, ksize=3)
            grad_y_prev = cv2.Sobel(prev_frame_gray, cv2.CV_64F, 0, 1, ksize=3)

            for y in range(0, frame_gray.shape[0] - block_size, block_size):
                for x in range(0, frame_gray.shape[1] - block_size, block_size):
                    min_cost = float('inf')
                    best_dx = 0
                    best_dy = 0
                    for dy in range(-search_range, search_range + 1):
                        for dx in range(-search_range, search_range + 1):
                            # Ensure the search area is within frame boundaries
                            if 0 <= y + dy < frame_gray.shape[0] - block_size and 0 <= x + dx < frame_gray.shape[1] - block_size:
                                template = prev_frame_gray[y:y+block_size, x:x+block_size]
                                search_area = frame_gray[y+dy:y+dy+block_size, x+dx:x+dx+block_size]

                                # Compute gradient of the search area
                                grad_x_search = cv2.Sobel(search_area, cv2.CV_64F, 1, 0, ksize=3)
                                grad_y_search = cv2.Sobel(search_area, cv2.CV_64F, 0, 1, ksize=3)

                                # Compute sum of squared differences of gradients
                                ssd_grad = np.sum((grad_x_prev[y:y+block_size, x:x+block_size] - grad_x_search)**2 + (grad_y_prev[y:y+block_size, x:x+block_size] - grad_y_search)**2)
                                if ssd_grad < min_cost:
                                    min_cost = ssd_grad
                                    best_dx = dx
                                    best_dy = dy
                    motion_vectors[y // block_size, x // block_size] = [best_dx, best_dy]
```

```python
        return motion_vectors

    def track_object(self, frame, bbox):
        if bbox:
            x1, y1, x2, y2 = map(int, bbox)
            roi = frame[y1:y2, x1:x2]
            if roi.size > 0:
                # Convert the ROI to grayscale
                roi_gray = cv2.cvtColor(roi, cv2.COLOR_BGR2GRAY)
                # Initialize the previous frame if not already initialized or if its dimensions don't match the current frame
                if self.prev_frame_gray is None or self.prev_frame_gray.shape != roi_gray.shape:
                    self.prev_frame_gray = roi_gray.copy()

                # Calculate motion vectors using gradient-based block matching
                motion_vectors = self.gradient_based_block_matching_pyramid(self.prev_frame_gray, roi_gray)

                # Calculate the mean motion vector within the bounding box
                mean_motion_vector = np.mean(motion_vectors, axis=(0, 1))

                # Update the bounding box coordinates based on the mean motion vector
                x1 += int(mean_motion_vector[0])
                y1 += int(mean_motion_vector[1])
                x2 += int(mean_motion_vector[0])
                y2 += int(mean_motion_vector[1])

                # Update the previous frame
                self.prev_frame_gray = roi_gray.copy()

                # Calculate the center of the bounding box
                center_x = (x1 + x2) // 2
                center_y = (y1 + y2) // 2

                # Add the center coordinates to the list box
                self.center_listbox.insert(tk.END, f"(center_x = {center_x}, center_y = {center_y})")

                return x1, y1, x2, y2
        return None
```

The gradient_based_block_matching_pyramid() method implements the Gradient-Based Block Matching Algorithm (GBBM) with a pyramid approach for motion estimation in consecutive video frames. This algorithm is essential for object tracking applications as it efficiently estimates the motion vectors of objects across frames, enabling accurate tracking.

The method begins by initializing the pyramid levels based on the value entered by the user. It constructs Gaussian pyramid representations of the previous and current frames to capture motion at multiple resolutions. This multiscale approach improves the robustness of motion estimation, particularly in scenarios with significant scale variations.

Next, it iterates over each pyramid level in reverse order, starting from the highest resolution. For each level, it adjusts the block size and search range parameters accordingly to account for the varying resolutions. This ensures that the algorithm effectively captures motion details across different scales.

Within each pyramid level, the method computes the gradient of the previous frame and iterates over blocks to search for the best matching block in the current frame. It calculates the sum of squared differences of gradients between the template block in the previous frame and the search area in the current frame.

The algorithm searches within a specified range of motion to find the block with the minimum gradient-based cost, indicating the best match. It updates the motion vectors with the displacement values that minimize the cost, representing the motion between the corresponding blocks in consecutive frames.

After completing the motion estimation process for all pyramid levels, the method returns the motion vectors representing the displacement of blocks between consecutive frames.

The track_object() method utilizes the motion vectors obtained from the pyramid-based block matching algorithm to track objects within the video frames. It calculates the mean motion vector within the bounding box of the tracked object and updates the bounding box coordinates accordingly.

Additionally, it maintains a list box to display the center coordinates of the tracked object in each frame, providing users with insights into the object's movement throughout the video.

Overall, these methods form the core of the object tracking functionality in the application, enabling accurate and robust tracking of objects in video sequences using the GBBM algorithm with a pyramid approach.

RUNNING PROGRAM

Run program and click on Open Video button. Then, choose a video file then click on Next Frame button.

SOURCE CODE

```
# object_tracking_gbbm_pyramid.py
import tkinter as tk
from tkinter import ttk
from tkinter import filedialog
from PIL import Image, ImageTk
import imageio
import cv2
import numpy as np

class ObjectTrackingGBBM_Pyramid:
```

```python
    def __init__(self, master):
        self.master = master
        self.master.title("Object Tracking with Gradient-Based Block Matching 
Algorithm (GBBM) with Pyramid Apporach")
        self.file_name = ""
        self.set_window_title()  # Set window title initially

        self.frame_number_label = tk.Label(master, text="Frame: 0")
        self.frame_number_label.pack()

        self.video = None
        self.video_path = None
        self.paused = False
        self.zoom_scale = tk.IntVar(value=1)
        self.frame_index = 0
        self.bbox = None
        self.tracking_started = False  # Initialize tracking_started to False
        self.prev_frame_gray = None

        self.bbox_rect = None  # Initialize bbox_rect attribute to None
        self.frame_processing = False  # Initialize frame_processing attribute to 
False

        self.create_widgets()

    def create_widgets(self):
        # Panel for video display
        video_panel = tk.Frame(self.master)
        video_panel.pack(padx=10, pady=10)

        # Canvas to display the original video
        canvas_width = 800
        canvas_height = 500
        self.canvas = tk.Canvas(video_panel, width=canvas_width, 
height=canvas_height)
        self.canvas.pack(side="left", fill="both", expand=True)
        self.canvas.bind("<MouseWheel>", self.on_mousewheel)
        self.canvas.bind("<ButtonPress-1>", self.on_press)
        self.canvas.bind("<B1-Motion>", self.on_drag)

        # List box to display center coordinates
        self.center_listbox = tk.Listbox(video_panel, width=30, height=20, 
font=("Helvetica", 14))
        self.center_listbox.pack(side="right", fill="y")
        # Scrollbar for the listbox
        scrollbar = tk.Scrollbar(video_panel, orient="vertical")
        scrollbar.pack(side="left", fill="y")
        scrollbar.config(command=self.center_listbox.yview)
```

```python
        # Attach scrollbar to listbox
        self.center_listbox.config(yscrollcommand=scrollbar.set)
        
        # Panel for control buttons
        control_panel = tk.Frame(self.master)
        control_panel.pack(padx=10, pady=(0, 10), fill="x")
        
        # Button to open a video file
        self.open_button = tk.Button(control_panel, text="Open Video", command=self.open_video)
        self.open_button.grid(row=0, column=0, padx=10, pady=5)
        
        # Combobox for selecting zoom scale
        self.zoom_combobox = ttk.Combobox(control_panel, textvariable=self.zoom_scale, values=list(range(1, 11)))
        self.zoom_combobox.grid(row=0, column=1, padx=10, pady=5)
        self.zoom_combobox.bind("<<ComboboxSelected>>", self.update_zoom)
        
        # Button to play/pause the video
        self.play_button = tk.Button(control_panel, text="Play/Pause", command=self.toggle_play_pause)
        self.play_button.grid(row=0, column=2, padx=10, pady=5)
        
        # Button to stop the video
        self.stop_button = tk.Button(control_panel, text="Stop", command=self.stop_video)
        self.stop_button.grid(row=0, column=3, padx=10, pady=5)
        
        # Button to navigate to the previous frame
        self.prev_frame_button = tk.Button(control_panel, text="Previous Frame", command=self.prev_frame)
        self.prev_frame_button.grid(row=0, column=4, padx=10, pady=5)
        
        # Button to navigate to the next frame
        self.next_frame_button = tk.Button(control_panel, text="Next Frame", command=self.next_frame)
        self.next_frame_button.grid(row=0, column=5, padx=10, pady=5)
        
        # Button to clear the listbox
        self.clear_button = tk.Button(control_panel, text="Clear Listbox", command=self.clear_listbox)
        self.clear_button.grid(row=0, column=6, padx=10, pady=5)
        
        # Label and entry for specifying block size
        self.block_size_label = tk.Label(control_panel, text="Block Size:")
        self.block_size_label.grid(row=0, column=7, padx=10, pady=5, sticky="e")
        self.block_size_default = tk.StringVar(value="8")
```

```python
        self.block_size_entry = ttk.Entry(control_panel, textvariable=self.block_size_default)
        self.block_size_entry.grid(row=0, column=8, padx=10, pady=5, sticky="w")
        self.block_size_entry.bind("<Return>", lambda event: self.toggle_play_pause())

        # Label and entry for specifying search range
        self.search_range_label = tk.Label(control_panel, text="Search Range:")
        self.search_range_label.grid(row=0, column=9, padx=10, pady=5, sticky="e")
        self.search_range_default = tk.StringVar(value="8")
        self.search_range_entry = ttk.Entry(control_panel, textvariable=self.search_range_default)
        self.search_range_entry.grid(row=0, column=10, padx=10, pady=5, sticky="w")
        self.search_range_entry.bind("<Return>", lambda event: self.toggle_play_pause())

        # Label and entry for specifying levels of pyramid
        self.level_label = tk.Label(control_panel, text="Level of Pyramid:")
        self.level_label.grid(row=1, column=1, padx=10, pady=5, sticky="e")
        self.level_default = tk.StringVar(value="2")
        self.level_entry = ttk.Entry(control_panel, textvariable=self.level_default)
        self.level_entry.grid(row=1, column=2, padx=10, pady=5, sticky="w")
        self.level_entry.bind("<Return>", lambda event: self.toggle_play_pause())

    def open_video(self):
        self.video_path = filedialog.askopenfilename(filetypes=[("Video files", "*.mp4;*.avi;*.mkv;*.wmv")])
        if self.video_path:
            self.video = imageio.get_reader(self.video_path)
            self.file_name = self.video_path.split('/')[-1]
            self.set_window_title()
            self.play_video()

    def play_video(self):
        if self.video:
            self.paused = False
            self.tracking_started = True
            self.show_frame()

    def stop_video(self):
        self.paused = True
        self.frame_index = 0
        self.bbox = None
        self.show_frame()

    def toggle_play_pause(self):
        self.paused = not self.paused
        if not self.paused:
```

```python
            if self.bbox is not None:
                self.tracking_started = True
            self.play_video()

    def update_zoom(self, event=None):
        self.show_frame()

    def gradient_based_block_matching_pyramid(self, prev_frame_gray, frame_gray):
        # Initialize pyramid levels
        levels = int(self.level_entry.get())
        pyramid_prev = [prev_frame_gray]
        pyramid_frame = [frame_gray]
        for _ in range(levels - 1):
            prev_frame_gray = cv2.pyrDown(prev_frame_gray)
            frame_gray = cv2.pyrDown(frame_gray)
            pyramid_prev.append(prev_frame_gray)
            pyramid_frame.append(frame_gray)

        block_size = int(self.block_size_entry.get())  # Get block size from entry
        search_range = int(self.search_range_entry.get())  # Get search range from entry
        motion_vectors = np.zeros((frame_gray.shape[0] // block_size, frame_gray.shape[1] // block_size, 2))

        for level in range(levels - 1, -1, -1):  # Iterate over pyramid levels in reverse order
            prev_frame_gray = pyramid_prev[level]
            frame_gray = pyramid_frame[level]
            block_size = block_size * (2 ** level)  # Adjust block size based on pyramid level
            search_range = search_range * (2 ** level)  # Adjust search range based on pyramid level

            # Compute gradient of the previous frame
            grad_x_prev = cv2.Sobel(prev_frame_gray, cv2.CV_64F, 1, 0, ksize=3)
            grad_y_prev = cv2.Sobel(prev_frame_gray, cv2.CV_64F, 0, 1, ksize=3)

            for y in range(0, frame_gray.shape[0] - block_size, block_size):
                for x in range(0, frame_gray.shape[1] - block_size, block_size):
                    min_cost = float('inf')
                    best_dx = 0
                    best_dy = 0
                    for dy in range(-search_range, search_range + 1):
                        for dx in range(-search_range, search_range + 1):
                            # Ensure the search area is within frame boundaries
                            if 0 <= y + dy < frame_gray.shape[0] - block_size and 0 <= x + dx < frame_gray.shape[1] - block_size:
```

```python
                            template = prev_frame_gray[y:y+block_size, x:x+block_size]
                            search_area = frame_gray[y+dy:y+dy+block_size, x+dx:x+dx+block_size]

                            # Compute gradient of the search area
                            grad_x_search = cv2.Sobel(search_area, cv2.CV_64F, 1, 0, ksize=3)
                            grad_y_search = cv2.Sobel(search_area, cv2.CV_64F, 0, 1, ksize=3)

                            # Compute sum of squared differences of gradients
                            ssd_grad = np.sum((grad_x_prev[y:y+block_size, x:x+block_size] - grad_x_search)**2 + (grad_y_prev[y:y+block_size, x:x+block_size] - grad_y_search)**2)
                            if ssd_grad < min_cost:
                                min_cost = ssd_grad
                                best_dx = dx
                                best_dy = dy
                    motion_vectors[y // block_size, x // block_size] = [best_dx, best_dy]

        return motion_vectors

    def track_object(self, frame, bbox):
        if bbox:
            x1, y1, x2, y2 = map(int, bbox)
            roi = frame[y1:y2, x1:x2]
            if roi.size > 0:
                # Convert the ROI to grayscale
                roi_gray = cv2.cvtColor(roi, cv2.COLOR_BGR2GRAY)
                # Initialize the previous frame if not already initialized or if its dimensions don't match the current frame
                if self.prev_frame_gray is None or self.prev_frame_gray.shape != roi_gray.shape:
                    self.prev_frame_gray = roi_gray.copy()

                # Calculate motion vectors using gradient-based block matching
                motion_vectors = self.gradient_based_block_matching_pyramid(self.prev_frame_gray, roi_gray)

                # Calculate the mean motion vector within the bounding box
                mean_motion_vector = np.mean(motion_vectors, axis=(0, 1))

                # Update the bounding box coordinates based on the mean motion vector
                x1 += int(mean_motion_vector[0])
                y1 += int(mean_motion_vector[1])
                x2 += int(mean_motion_vector[0])
```

```python
                    y2 += int(mean_motion_vector[1])

                    # Update the previous frame
                    self.prev_frame_gray = roi_gray.copy()

                    # Calculate the center of the bounding box
                    center_x = (x1 + x2) // 2
                    center_y = (y1 + y2) // 2

                    # Add the center coordinates to the list box
                    self.center_listbox.insert(tk.END, f"(center_x = {center_x}, center_y = {center_y})")

                    return x1, y1, x2, y2
        return None

    def update_bbox_rectangle(self, bbox):
        if bbox is not None:
            x1, y1, x2, y2 = map(int, bbox)
            if self.bbox_rect is not None:
                self.canvas.coords(self.bbox_rect, x1, y1, x2, y2)
                self.canvas.tag_raise(self.bbox_rect)  # Raise the bounding box to the front
            else:
                self.bbox_rect = self.canvas.create_rectangle(x1, y1, x2-50, y2-50, outline='#fc3d3d', width=8, tags="bbox")

    def show_frame(self):
        if self.video:
            if not self.paused:
                if 0 <= self.frame_index < len(self.video):
                    if not self.frame_processing:  # Check if the frame is already being processed
                        try:
                            self.frame_processing = True  # Set frame_processing flag to True to indicate frame processing

                            frame = self.video.get_data(self.frame_index)
                            frame = cv2.cvtColor(frame, cv2.COLOR_RGB2BGR)

                            if self.bbox is not None:
                                if not self.tracking_started:
                                    self.tracking_started = True

                                self.bbox = self.track_object(frame, self.bbox)
                                if self.bbox:
                                    frame = cv2.cvtColor(frame, cv2.COLOR_BGR2RGB)
                                    frame = Image.fromarray(frame)
```

```
                                    frame = frame.resize((frame.width * 
self.zoom_scale.get(), frame.height * self.zoom_scale.get()))
                                    photo = ImageTk.PhotoImage(frame)
                                    self.photo = photo
                                    self.canvas.delete("video")
                                    self.canvas.create_image(0, 0, anchor="nw", 
image=photo, tags="video")

                                    self.update_bbox_rectangle(self.bbox)

                                else:
                                    frame = cv2.cvtColor(frame, cv2.COLOR_BGR2RGB)
                                    frame = Image.fromarray(frame)
                                    frame = frame.resize((frame.width * 
self.zoom_scale.get(), frame.height * self.zoom_scale.get()))
                                    photo = ImageTk.PhotoImage(frame)
                                    self.photo = photo
                                    self.canvas.delete("video")
                                    self.canvas.create_image(0, 0, anchor="nw", 
image=photo, tags="video")

                                self.frame_number_label.config(text=f"Frame: 
{self.frame_index} / {self.video.count_frames()}", font=("Helvetica", 18))

                                self.frame_index += 1

                    except Exception as e:
                        print("Error: ", e)
                    finally:
                        self.frame_processing = False  # Reset frame_processing 
flag to False after processing the frame

    def on_mousewheel(self, event):
        direction = event.delta // 120
        current_value = int(self.zoom_scale.get())
        if direction == 1 and current_value < 10:
            current_value += 1
        elif direction == -1 and current_value > 1:
            current_value -= 1
        self.zoom_scale.set(current_value)
        self.update_zoom()

    def on_press(self, event):
        self.start_x = self.canvas.canvasx(event.x)
        self.start_y = self.canvas.canvasy(event.y)
        self.bbox = None

    def on_drag(self, event):
        cur_x = self.canvas.canvasx(event.x)
```

```python
            cur_y = self.canvas.canvasy(event.y)
            if self.bbox_rect:
                self.canvas.delete(self.bbox_rect)
            self.bbox = (self.start_x, self.start_y, cur_x, cur_y)
            self.bbox_rect = self.canvas.create_rectangle(*self.bbox, outline='#fc3d3d', width=6)

    def prev_frame(self):
        if self.frame_index > 0:
            self.frame_index -= 1
            self.show_frame()

    def next_frame(self):
        if self.video and self.frame_index < len(self.video) - 1:
            self.show_frame()

    def clear_listbox(self):
        self.center_listbox.delete(0, tk.END)

    def set_window_title(self):
        if self.file_name:
            self.master.title(f"Object Tracking with Gradient-Based Block Matching Algorithm (GBBM) with Pyramid Apporach - {self.file_name}")
            self.master.title_font = ("Helvetica", 16, "bold")
        else:
            self.master.title("Object Tracking with Gradient-Based Block Matching Algorithm (GBBM) with Pyramid Apporach")

def main():
    root = tk.Tk()
    app = ObjectTrackingGBBM_Pyramid(root)
    root.mainloop()

if __name__ == "__main__":
    main()
```

OBJECT TRACKING WITH GRADIENT-BASED BLOCK MATCHING ALGORITHM (GBBM) WITH ADAPTIVE BLOCK SIZE

DESCRIPTION

The purpose of the "Object Tracking with Gradient-Based Block Matching Algorithm (GBBM) with Adaptive Block Size" project is to develop a graphical user interface (GUI) application that allows users to track objects in video files using computer vision techniques. The project utilizes the GBBM algorithm, a widely used method for motion estimation in video processing, to track objects efficiently across consecutive frames.

The project aims to provide users with a user-friendly interface for loading video files, playing/pausing video playback, navigating through frames, and tracking objects in real-time. The GUI allows users to interact with the video frames, adjust the zoom scale for better visualization, and monitor the center coordinates of the tracked object throughout the video sequence.

The application leverages the adaptive block size variant of the GBBM algorithm to enhance the accuracy and robustness of object tracking. By dynamically adjusting the block size based on the gradient magnitude of the video frames, the algorithm can adapt to changes in object size and motion, improving tracking performance in various scenarios.

One of the primary goals of the project is to simplify the process of object tracking for users with limited programming experience. By providing a intuitive GUI interface, users can easily load video files, define bounding boxes around objects of interest, and visualize the tracking results in real-time.

The project also serves as a learning tool for individuals interested in computer vision and video processing. By examining the source code and understanding the implementation of the GBBM algorithm with adaptive block size, users can gain insights into motion estimation techniques and their applications in object tracking.

Furthermore, the project aims to demonstrate the practical applications of computer vision algorithms in real-world scenarios such as surveillance, video analysis, and human-computer interaction. By showcasing the capabilities of the GBBM algorithm, the application highlights the potential of computer vision technology in various domains.

The project fosters collaboration and knowledge sharing within the computer vision community by providing an open-source implementation of the GBBM algorithm with adaptive block size. Developers and researchers can contribute to the project, enhance its functionality, and adapt it to specific use cases or environments.

Moreover, the project encourages experimentation and exploration by allowing users to customize parameters such as block size and search range for motion estimation. By fine-tuning these parameters, users can optimize the tracking performance based on the characteristics of the video content and the objects being tracked.

Overall, the "Object Tracking with Gradient-Based Block Matching Algorithm (GBBM) with Adaptive Block Size" project aims to empower users with a versatile tool for object tracking in video files, facilitate learning and research in computer vision, and promote innovation in the field of video processing and analysis. Through its intuitive interface and robust algorithmic foundation, the project strives to make object tracking accessible, efficient, and reliable for a wide range of applications and users.

TRACKING OBJECT

```python
    def gradient_based_block_matching_adaptive(self, prev_frame_gray, frame_gray):
        # GBBM implementation with adaptive block size
        search_range = int(self.search_range_entry.get())  # Get search range from entry
        block_size = int(self.block_size_entry.get())  # Get block size from entry
        motion_vectors = np.zeros((frame_gray.shape[0] // block_size, frame_gray.shape[1] // block_size, 2))

        # Compute gradient magnitude of the previous frame
        grad_x_search = cv2.Sobel(prev_frame_gray, cv2.CV_64F, 1, 0, ksize=3)
        grad_y_search = cv2.Sobel(prev_frame_gray, cv2.CV_64F, 0, 1, ksize=3)
        grad_mag_prev = np.sqrt(grad_x_search ** 2 + grad_y_search ** 2)

        for y in range(0, frame_gray.shape[0] - block_size + 1, block_size):
            for x in range(0, frame_gray.shape[1] - block_size + 1, block_size):
                # Calculate average gradient magnitude within the block
                block_grad_mag = grad_mag_prev[y:y+block_size, x:x+block_size]
                avg_grad_mag = np.mean(block_grad_mag)

                # Calculate adaptive block size based on average gradient magnitude
                adaptive_block_size = int(16 * (1 + avg_grad_mag / 255))  # Adjust the factor as needed

                min_cost = float('inf')
                best_dx = 0
                best_dy = 0
                for dy in range(-search_range, search_range + 1):
                    for dx in range(-search_range, search_range + 1):
                        # Ensure the search area is within block boundaries
                        if 0 <= y + dy < frame_gray.shape[0] - block_size and 0 <= x + dx < frame_gray.shape[1] - block_size:
                            grad_mag_search = np.sqrt(grad_x_search ** 2 + grad_y_search ** 2)

                            # Resize grad_mag_prev to match the size of the current block
                            grad_mag_search = cv2.resize(grad_mag_search, (block_size, block_size))

                            # Compute sum of squared differences of gradients
```

```python
                        ssd_grad = np.sum((block_grad_mag - grad_mag_search) ** 2)

                        if ssd_grad < min_cost:
                            min_cost = ssd_grad
                            best_dx = dx
                            best_dy = dy
                    motion_vectors[y // block_size, x // block_size] = [best_dx, best_dy]

        return motion_vectors

    def track_object(self, frame, bbox):
        if bbox:
            x1, y1, x2, y2 = map(int, bbox)
            roi = frame[y1:y2, x1:x2]
            if roi.size > 0:
                # Convert the ROI to grayscale
                roi_gray = cv2.cvtColor(roi, cv2.COLOR_BGR2GRAY)
                # Initialize the previous frame if not already initialized or if its dimensions don't match the current frame
                if self.prev_frame_gray is None or self.prev_frame_gray.shape != roi_gray.shape:
                    self.prev_frame_gray = roi_gray.copy()

                # Calculate motion vectors using gradient-based block matching with adaptive block size
                motion_vectors = self.gradient_based_block_matching_adaptive(self.prev_frame_gray, roi_gray)

                # Calculate the mean motion vector within the bounding box
                mean_motion_vector = np.mean(motion_vectors, axis=(0, 1))

                # Update the bounding box coordinates based on the mean motion vector
                x1 += int(mean_motion_vector[0])
                y1 += int(mean_motion_vector[1])
                x2 += int(mean_motion_vector[0])
                y2 += int(mean_motion_vector[1])

                # Update the previous frame
                self.prev_frame_gray = roi_gray.copy()

                # Calculate the center of the bounding box
                center_x = (x1 + x2) // 2
                center_y = (y1 + y2) // 2

                # Add the center coordinates to the list box
                self.center_listbox.insert(tk.END, f"(center_x = {center_x}, center_y = {center_y})")
```

```
            return x1, y1, x2, y2
    return None
```

In the gradient_based_block_matching_adaptive() method, the gradient-based block matching algorithm with adaptive block size is implemented. This algorithm is used to estimate motion vectors between the previous frame (prev_frame_gray) and the current frame (frame_gray). Here's how it works:
1. Initialization: The method initializes parameters such as search range and block size by retrieving them from the GUI entry widgets (search_range_entry and block_size_entry, respectively). It also initializes a numpy array to store the motion vectors.
2. Gradient Calculation: Sobel operators are applied to the previous frame (prev_frame_gray) to compute the gradient in both the x and y directions. These gradients are then combined to obtain the gradient magnitude of the previous frame.
3. Block Iteration: The method iterates over blocks of pixels in the current frame (frame_gray). For each block, it calculates the average gradient magnitude within that block and computes an adaptive block size based on this average magnitude.
4. Motion Estimation: Within each block, a search is performed to find the most similar block in the previous frame. The search is conducted within a specified search range. For each candidate motion vector, the sum of squared differences (SSD) of gradients between the current block and the corresponding block in the previous frame is computed.
5. Motion Vector Selection: The motion vector with the lowest SSD of gradients is selected as the best match. This vector represents the estimated motion between the current block and the corresponding block in the previous frame.
6. Motion Vector Storage: The computed motion vectors are stored in the motion_vectors array.

The track_object() method utilizes the gradient_based_block_matching_adaptive() method to estimate motion vectors between the current frame region of interest (ROI) and the corresponding region in the previous frame. Here's a breakdown:
1. ROI Extraction: The method extracts the region of interest (ROI) from the current frame based on the provided bounding box (bbox).
2. ROI Conversion: The ROI is converted to grayscale (roi_gray) using OpenCV's cvtColor function.

3. Initialization and Comparison: If the previous frame (prev_frame_gray) is not initialized or its dimensions don't match the ROI, it is initialized or updated accordingly. This ensures consistency in motion estimation.
4. Motion Estimation: The gradient_based_block_matching_adaptive method is called to estimate motion vectors between the ROI and the corresponding region in the previous frame.
5. Mean Motion Vector Calculation: The mean motion vector is calculated by averaging the motion vectors within the ROI.
6. Bounding Box Update: The bounding box coordinates (x1, y1, x2, y2) are updated based on the mean motion vector.
7. Previous Frame Update: The previous frame (prev_frame_gray) is updated with the current ROI.
8. Center Calculation and Display: The center coordinates of the updated bounding box are calculated, and a string representing these coordinates is added to the list box (center_listbox) for visualization.
9. Return: The updated bounding box coordinates are returned for further processing or visualization.

The track_object() method thus facilitates object tracking by estimating motion vectors and updating bounding box coordinates based on these estimates.

RUNNING PROGRAM

Run program and click on Open Video button. Then, choose a video file then click on Next Frame button.

SOURCE CODE

```python
# object_tracking_gbbm_adaptive.py
import tkinter as tk
from tkinter import ttk
from tkinter import filedialog
from PIL import Image, ImageTk
import imageio
import cv2
import numpy as np

class ObjectTrackingGBBM_Adaptive:
    def __init__(self, master):
        self.master = master
        self.master.title("Object Tracking with Gradient-Based Block Matching Algorithm (GBBM) with Adaptive Block Size")
        self.file_name = ""
        self.set_window_title()  # Set window title initially

        self.frame_number_label = tk.Label(master, text="Frame: 0")
```

```python
        self.frame_number_label.pack()

        self.video = None
        self.video_path = None
        self.paused = False
        self.zoom_scale = tk.IntVar(value=1)
        self.frame_index = 0
        self.bbox = None
        self.tracking_started = False  # Initialize tracking_started to False
        self.prev_frame_gray = None

        self.bbox_rect = None  # Initialize bbox_rect attribute to None
        self.frame_processing = False  # Initialize frame_processing attribute to False

        self.create_widgets()

    def create_widgets(self):
        # Panel for video display
        video_panel = tk.Frame(self.master)
        video_panel.pack(padx=10, pady=10)

        # Canvas to display the original video
        canvas_width = 800
        canvas_height = 500
        self.canvas = tk.Canvas(video_panel, width=canvas_width, height=canvas_height)
        self.canvas.pack(side="left", fill="both", expand=True)
        self.canvas.bind("<MouseWheel>", self.on_mousewheel)
        self.canvas.bind("<ButtonPress-1>", self.on_press)
        self.canvas.bind("<B1-Motion>", self.on_drag)

        # List box to display center coordinates
        self.center_listbox = tk.Listbox(video_panel, width=30, height=20, font=("Helvetica", 14))
        self.center_listbox.pack(side="right", fill="y")
        # Scrollbar for the listbox
        scrollbar = tk.Scrollbar(video_panel, orient="vertical")
        scrollbar.pack(side="left", fill="y")
        scrollbar.config(command=self.center_listbox.yview)

        # Attach scrollbar to listbox
        self.center_listbox.config(yscrollcommand=scrollbar.set)

        # Panel for control buttons
        control_panel = tk.Frame(self.master)
        control_panel.pack(padx=10, pady=(0, 10), fill="x")
```

```python
        # Button to open a video file
        self.open_button = tk.Button(control_panel, text="Open Video", command=self.open_video)
        self.open_button.grid(row=0, column=0, padx=10, pady=5)

        # Combobox for selecting zoom scale
        self.zoom_combobox = ttk.Combobox(control_panel, textvariable=self.zoom_scale, values=list(range(1, 11)))
        self.zoom_combobox.grid(row=0, column=1, padx=10, pady=5)
        self.zoom_combobox.bind("<<ComboboxSelected>>", self.update_zoom)

        # Button to play/pause the video
        self.play_button = tk.Button(control_panel, text="Play/Pause", command=self.toggle_play_pause)
        self.play_button.grid(row=0, column=2, padx=10, pady=5)

        # Button to stop the video
        self.stop_button = tk.Button(control_panel, text="Stop", command=self.stop_video)
        self.stop_button.grid(row=0, column=3, padx=10, pady=5)

        # Button to navigate to the previous frame
        self.prev_frame_button = tk.Button(control_panel, text="Previous Frame", command=self.prev_frame)
        self.prev_frame_button.grid(row=0, column=4, padx=10, pady=5)

        # Button to navigate to the next frame
        self.next_frame_button = tk.Button(control_panel, text="Next Frame", command=self.next_frame)
        self.next_frame_button.grid(row=0, column=5, padx=10, pady=5)

        # Button to clear the listbox
        self.clear_button = tk.Button(control_panel, text="Clear Listbox", command=self.clear_listbox)
        self.clear_button.grid(row=0, column=6, padx=10, pady=5)

        # Label and entry for specifying block size
        self.block_size_label = tk.Label(control_panel, text="Block Size:")
        self.block_size_label.grid(row=0, column=7, padx=10, pady=5, sticky="e")
        self.block_size_default = tk.StringVar(value="8")
        self.block_size_entry = ttk.Entry(control_panel, textvariable=self.block_size_default)
        self.block_size_entry.grid(row=0, column=8, padx=10, pady=5, sticky="w")
        self.block_size_entry.bind("<Return>", lambda event: self.toggle_play_pause())

        # Label and entry for specifying search range
        self.search_range_label = tk.Label(control_panel, text="Search Range:")
```

```python
        self.search_range_label.grid(row=0, column=9, padx=10, pady=5, sticky="e")
        self.search_range_default = tk.StringVar(value="8")
        self.search_range_entry = ttk.Entry(control_panel, textvariable=self.search_range_default)
        self.search_range_entry.grid(row=0, column=10, padx=10, pady=5, sticky="w")
        self.search_range_entry.bind("<Return>", lambda event: self.toggle_play_pause())

    def open_video(self):
        self.video_path = filedialog.askopenfilename(filetypes=[("Video files", "*.mp4;*.avi;*.mkv;*.wmv")])
        if self.video_path:
            self.video = imageio.get_reader(self.video_path)
            self.file_name = self.video_path.split('/')[-1]
            self.set_window_title()
            self.play_video()

    def play_video(self):
        if self.video:
            self.paused = False
            self.tracking_started = True
            self.show_frame()

    def stop_video(self):
        self.paused = True
        self.frame_index = 0
        self.bbox = None
        self.show_frame()

    def toggle_play_pause(self):
        self.paused = not self.paused
        if not self.paused:
            if self.bbox is not None:
                self.tracking_started = True
            self.play_video()

    def update_zoom(self, event=None):
        self.show_frame()

    def gradient_based_block_matching_adaptive(self, prev_frame_gray, frame_gray):
        # GBBM implementation with adaptive block size
        search_range = int(self.search_range_entry.get())  # Get search range from entry
        block_size = int(self.block_size_entry.get())  # Get block size from entry
        motion_vectors = np.zeros((frame_gray.shape[0] // block_size, frame_gray.shape[1] // block_size, 2))

        # Compute gradient magnitude of the previous frame
```

```python
            grad_x_search = cv2.Sobel(prev_frame_gray, cv2.CV_64F, 1, 0, ksize=3)
            grad_y_search = cv2.Sobel(prev_frame_gray, cv2.CV_64F, 0, 1, ksize=3)
            grad_mag_prev = np.sqrt(grad_x_search ** 2 + grad_y_search ** 2)

            for y in range(0, frame_gray.shape[0] - block_size + 1, block_size):
                for x in range(0, frame_gray.shape[1] - block_size + 1, block_size):
                    # Calculate average gradient magnitude within the block
                    block_grad_mag = grad_mag_prev[y:y+block_size, x:x+block_size]
                    avg_grad_mag = np.mean(block_grad_mag)

                    # Calculate adaptive block size based on average gradient magnitude
                    adaptive_block_size = int(16 * (1 + avg_grad_mag / 255))   # Adjust the factor as needed

                    min_cost = float('inf')
                    best_dx = 0
                    best_dy = 0
                    for dy in range(-search_range, search_range + 1):
                        for dx in range(-search_range, search_range + 1):
                            # Ensure the search area is within block boundaries
                            if 0 <= y + dy < frame_gray.shape[0] - block_size and 0 <= x + dx < frame_gray.shape[1] - block_size:
                                grad_mag_search = np.sqrt(grad_x_search ** 2 + grad_y_search ** 2)

                                # Resize grad_mag_prev to match the size of the current block
                                grad_mag_search = cv2.resize(grad_mag_search, (block_size, block_size))

                                # Compute sum of squared differences of gradients
                                ssd_grad = np.sum((block_grad_mag - grad_mag_search) ** 2)

                                if ssd_grad < min_cost:
                                    min_cost = ssd_grad
                                    best_dx = dx
                                    best_dy = dy
                    motion_vectors[y // block_size, x // block_size] = [best_dx, best_dy]

        return motion_vectors

    def track_object(self, frame, bbox):
        if bbox:
            x1, y1, x2, y2 = map(int, bbox)
            roi = frame[y1:y2, x1:x2]
            if roi.size > 0:
                # Convert the ROI to grayscale
```

```python
                roi_gray = cv2.cvtColor(roi, cv2.COLOR_BGR2GRAY)
                # Initialize the previous frame if not already initialized or if its 
dimensions don't match the current frame
                if self.prev_frame_gray is None or self.prev_frame_gray.shape != 
roi_gray.shape:
                    self.prev_frame_gray = roi_gray.copy()

                # Calculate motion vectors using gradient-based block matching with 
adaptive block size
                motion_vectors = 
self.gradient_based_block_matching_adaptive(self.prev_frame_gray, roi_gray)

                # Calculate the mean motion vector within the bounding box
                mean_motion_vector = np.mean(motion_vectors, axis=(0, 1))

                # Update the bounding box coordinates based on the mean motion vector
                x1 += int(mean_motion_vector[0])
                y1 += int(mean_motion_vector[1])
                x2 += int(mean_motion_vector[0])
                y2 += int(mean_motion_vector[1])

                # Update the previous frame
                self.prev_frame_gray = roi_gray.copy()

                # Calculate the center of the bounding box
                center_x = (x1 + x2) // 2
                center_y = (y1 + y2) // 2

                # Add the center coordinates to the list box
                self.center_listbox.insert(tk.END, f"(center_x = {center_x}, center_y 
= {center_y})")

                return x1, y1, x2, y2
        return None

    def update_bbox_rectangle(self, bbox):
        if bbox is not None:
            x1, y1, x2, y2 = map(int, bbox)
            if self.bbox_rect is not None:
                self.canvas.coords(self.bbox_rect, x1, y1, x2, y2)
                self.canvas.tag_raise(self.bbox_rect)  # Raise the bounding box to 
the front
            else:
                self.bbox_rect = self.canvas.create_rectangle(x1, y1, x2-50, y2-50, 
outline='#fc3d3d', width=8, tags="bbox")

    def show_frame(self):
        if self.video:
```

```python
            if not self.paused:
                if 0 <= self.frame_index < len(self.video):
                    if not self.frame_processing:  # Check if the frame is already being processed
                        try:
                            self.frame_processing = True  # Set frame_processing flag to True to indicate frame processing

                            frame = self.video.get_data(self.frame_index)
                            frame = cv2.cvtColor(frame, cv2.COLOR_RGB2BGR)

                            if self.bbox is not None:
                                if not self.tracking_started:
                                    self.tracking_started = True

                                self.bbox = self.track_object(frame, self.bbox)
                                if self.bbox:
                                    frame = cv2.cvtColor(frame, cv2.COLOR_BGR2RGB)
                                    frame = Image.fromarray(frame)
                                    frame = frame.resize((frame.width * self.zoom_scale.get(), frame.height * self.zoom_scale.get()))
                                    photo = ImageTk.PhotoImage(frame)
                                    self.photo = photo
                                    self.canvas.delete("video")
                                    self.canvas.create_image(0, 0, anchor="nw", image=photo, tags="video")

                                    self.update_bbox_rectangle(self.bbox)

                            else:
                                frame = cv2.cvtColor(frame, cv2.COLOR_BGR2RGB)
                                frame = Image.fromarray(frame)
                                frame = frame.resize((frame.width * self.zoom_scale.get(), frame.height * self.zoom_scale.get()))
                                photo = ImageTk.PhotoImage(frame)
                                self.photo = photo
                                self.canvas.delete("video")
                                self.canvas.create_image(0, 0, anchor="nw", image=photo, tags="video")

                            self.frame_number_label.config(text=f"Frame: {self.frame_index} / {self.video.count_frames()}", font=("Helvetica", 18))

                            self.frame_index += 1

                        except Exception as e:
                            print("Error: ", e)
                        finally:
```

```python
                            self.frame_processing = False  # Reset frame_processing 
flag to False after processing the frame

    def on_mousewheel(self, event):
        direction = event.delta // 120
        current_value = int(self.zoom_scale.get())
        if direction == 1 and current_value < 10:
            current_value += 1
        elif direction == -1 and current_value > 1:
            current_value -= 1
        self.zoom_scale.set(current_value)
        self.update_zoom()

    def on_press(self, event):
        self.start_x = self.canvas.canvasx(event.x)
        self.start_y = self.canvas.canvasy(event.y)
        self.bbox = None

    def on_drag(self, event):
        cur_x = self.canvas.canvasx(event.x)
        cur_y = self.canvas.canvasy(event.y)
        if self.bbox_rect:
            self.canvas.delete(self.bbox_rect)
        self.bbox = (self.start_x, self.start_y, cur_x, cur_y)
        self.bbox_rect = self.canvas.create_rectangle(*self.bbox, outline='#fc3d3d', 
width=6)

    def prev_frame(self):
        if self.frame_index > 0:
            self.frame_index -= 1
            self.show_frame()

    def next_frame(self):
        if self.video and self.frame_index < len(self.video) - 1:
            self.show_frame()

    def clear_listbox(self):
        self.center_listbox.delete(0, tk.END)

    def set_window_title(self):
        if self.file_name:
            self.master.title(f"Object Tracking with Gradient-Based Block Matching 
Algorithm (GBBM) with Adaptive Block Size - {self.file_name}")
            self.master.title_font = ("Helvetica", 16, "bold")
        else:
            self.master.title("Object Tracking with Gradient-Based Block Matching 
Algorithm (GBBM) with Adaptive Block Size")
```

```python
def main():
    root = tk.Tk()
    app = ObjectTrackingGBBM_Adaptive(root)
    root.mainloop()

if __name__ == "__main__":
    main()
```

OBJECT TRACKING WITH SCALE-INVARIANT FEATURE TRANSFORM (SIFT)

DESCRIPTION

This project, named "Object Tracking with SIFT Algorithm," is a graphical user interface (GUI) application developed using Python's tkinter library. The application is designed to track objects within a video using the Scale-Invariant Feature Transform (SIFT) algorithm.

Upon launching the application, the user is presented with a window containing several widgets. The main components of the GUI include a panel for displaying the video, a list box for showing the center coordinates of the tracked object, and a control panel with buttons for various functionalities.

The "Open Video" button allows the user to select a video file (supported formats include mp4, avi, mkv, and wmv) from their local system. Once a video is loaded, it is displayed in the canvas widget within the GUI.

The user can control the playback of the video using buttons such as "Play/Pause," "Stop," "Previous Frame," and "Next Frame." These buttons enable the user to navigate through the video frames and play, pause, or stop the video playback as desired.

The GUI also features a zoom combobox, which allows the user to adjust the zoom scale of the video display. This feature enhances the user experience by providing the flexibility to zoom in or out on the video frames.

The SIFT algorithm is employed for object tracking within the video frames. The algorithm detects and matches keypoints between consecutive frames, allowing for the estimation of motion vectors representing the movement of the tracked object. These motion vectors are then used to update the bounding box coordinates of the tracked object in real-time.

As the video is played, the application continuously tracks the object and updates the bounding box accordingly. The center coordinates of the bounding box are displayed in the list box, providing a visual representation of the object's trajectory throughout the video.

Additionally, the GUI allows the user to manually define a bounding box around the object of interest by clicking and dragging the mouse cursor over the video canvas. This feature enables the user to initiate object tracking from a specified region within the video frame.

Overall, the "Object Tracking with SIFT Algorithm" application provides a user-friendly interface for tracking objects in videos using the SIFT algorithm, offering both automated and manual control options for object selection and tracking.

TRACKING OBJECT

```python
    def sift_vectors(self, prev_frame_gray, frame_gray):
        sift = cv2.xfeatures2d.SIFT_create()
        keypoints_prev, descriptors_prev = sift.detectAndCompute(prev_frame_gray, None)
        keypoints_frame, descriptors_frame = sift.detectAndCompute(frame_gray, None)

        # Create BFMatcher object
        bf = cv2.BFMatcher()
```

```python
        # Match descriptors
        matches = bf.knnMatch(descriptors_prev, descriptors_frame, k=2)

        # Apply ratio test
        good_matches = []
        for m, n in matches:
            if m.distance < 0.75 * n.distance:
                good_matches.append(m)

        # Check if there are enough good matches
        if len(good_matches) < 2:
            return np.zeros((1, 2))  # Return zero motion vector if there are not enough good matches

        # Estimate motion vectors from good matches
        motion_vectors = np.zeros((len(good_matches), 2))
        for i, match in enumerate(good_matches):
            # Get the keypoints for the matched points
            prev_point = keypoints_prev[match.queryIdx].pt
            frame_point = keypoints_frame[match.trainIdx].pt

            # Calculate the motion vector
            dx = frame_point[0] - prev_point[0]
            dy = frame_point[1] - prev_point[1]

            # Store the motion vector
            motion_vectors[i] = [dx, dy]

        return motion_vectors

    def track_object(self, frame, bbox):
        if bbox:
            x1, y1, x2, y2 = map(int, bbox)
            roi = frame[y1:y2, x1:x2]
            if roi.size > 0:
                # Convert the ROI to grayscale
                roi_gray = cv2.cvtColor(roi, cv2.COLOR_BGR2GRAY)
                # Initialize the previous frame if not already initialized or if its dimensions don't match the current frame
                if self.prev_frame_gray is None or self.prev_frame_gray.shape != roi_gray.shape:
                    self.prev_frame_gray = roi_gray.copy()

                # Calculate motion vectors using SIFT Algorithm
                motion_vectors = self.sift_vectors(self.prev_frame_gray, roi_gray)

                # Calculate the mean motion vector within the bounding box
```

```
            mean_motion_vector = np.mean(motion_vectors, axis=0)

            # Update the bounding box coordinates based on the mean motion vector
            x1 += int(mean_motion_vector[0])
            y1 += int(mean_motion_vector[1])
            x2 += int(mean_motion_vector[0])
            y2 += int(mean_motion_vector[1])

            # Update the previous frame
            self.prev_frame_gray = roi_gray.copy()

            # Calculate the center of the bounding box
            center_x = (x1 + x2) // 2
            center_y = (y1 + y2) // 2

            # Add the center coordinates to the list box
            self.center_listbox.insert(tk.END, f"(center_x = {center_x}, center_y = {center_y})")

            return x1, y1, x2, y2
        return None
```

The sift_vectors() method is responsible for estimating motion vectors using the Scale-Invariant Feature Transform (SIFT) algorithm. Here's how it works:

1. SIFT keypoints and descriptors are computed for both the previous and current frames. This is achieved using the cv2.xfeatures2d.SIFT_create() method to create a SIFT object, followed by the detectAndCompute method to find keypoints and compute descriptors for each frame.
2. A Brute-Force Matcher object (bf) is created using cv2.BFMatcher().
3. Descriptors from the previous frame are matched with descriptors from the current frame using the knnMatch method, which returns k best matches for each descriptor.
4. A ratio test is applied to select only the "good" matches. For each pair of matches (m, n), if the distance of the closest match m is less than 0.75 times the distance of the second closest match n, then m is considered a good match and added to the list of good_matches.
5. If there are fewer than 2 good matches, indicating insufficient reliable data for motion estimation, a zero motion vector is returned.
6. Otherwise, motion vectors are estimated from the good matches. For each good match, the motion vector is calculated as the difference in coordinates between the matched keypoints in the previous and current frames.

7. The calculated motion vectors are stored in a NumPy array and returned.

The track_object() method utilizes the motion vectors obtained from sift_vectors to track the object within the bounding box:
1. If a bounding box (bbox) is provided, indicating the region of interest within the frame, the method proceeds to track the object.
2. The region of interest (ROI) corresponding to the bounding box is extracted from the current frame.
3. The ROI is converted to grayscale to prepare it for motion estimation.
4. If the previous frame is not yet initialized or its dimensions do not match the current ROI, the previous frame is initialized with a copy of the current ROI.
5. Motion vectors are calculated using the sift_vectors method, passing the previous grayscale frame and the current ROI.
6. The mean motion vector is computed from the obtained motion vectors.
7. The bounding box coordinates are updated based on the mean motion vector, effectively shifting the bounding box to track the object's movement.
8. The previous frame is updated with a copy of the current ROI.
9. The center coordinates of the updated bounding box are calculated and added to the list box for visualization.
10. Finally, the updated bounding box coordinates are returned.
11. If no bounding box is provided, indicating that object tracking has not yet started or the object is not visible in the frame, None is returned.

RUNNING PROGRAM

Run program and click on Open Video button. Then, choose a video file then click on Next Frame button.

SOURCE CODE

```python
# object_tracking_sift.py
import tkinter as tk
from tkinter import ttk
from tkinter import filedialog
from PIL import Image, ImageTk
import imageio
import cv2
import numpy as np

class ObjectTrackingSIFT:
    def __init__(self, master):
        self.master = master
        self.master.title("Object Tracking with SIFT Algorithm")
        self.file_name = ""
        self.set_window_title()  # Set window title initially

        self.frame_number_label = tk.Label(master, text="Frame: 0")
        self.frame_number_label.pack()

        self.video = None
        self.video_path = None
        self.paused = False
        self.zoom_scale = tk.IntVar(value=1)
        self.frame_index = 0
        self.bbox = None
        self.tracking_started = False  # Initialize tracking_started to False
        self.prev_frame_gray = None

        self.bbox_rect = None  # Initialize bbox_rect attribute to None
        self.frame_processing = False  # Initialize frame_processing attribute to False

        self.create_widgets()

    def create_widgets(self):
        # Panel for video display
        video_panel = tk.Frame(self.master)
        video_panel.pack(padx=10, pady=10)

        # Canvas to display the original video
        canvas_width = 800
        canvas_height = 500
        self.canvas = tk.Canvas(video_panel, width=canvas_width, height=canvas_height)
        self.canvas.pack(side="left", fill="both", expand=True)
```

```python
        self.canvas.bind("<MouseWheel>", self.on_mousewheel)
        self.canvas.bind("<ButtonPress-1>", self.on_press)
        self.canvas.bind("<B1-Motion>", self.on_drag)

        # List box to display center coordinates
        self.center_listbox = tk.Listbox(video_panel, width=30, height=20, font=("Helvetica", 14))
        self.center_listbox.pack(side="right", fill="y")
        # Scrollbar for the listbox
        scrollbar = tk.Scrollbar(video_panel, orient="vertical")
        scrollbar.pack(side="left", fill="y")
        scrollbar.config(command=self.center_listbox.yview)

        # Attach scrollbar to listbox
        self.center_listbox.config(yscrollcommand=scrollbar.set)

        # Panel for control buttons
        control_panel = tk.Frame(self.master)
        control_panel.pack(padx=10, pady=(0, 10), fill="x")

        # Button to open a video file
        self.open_button = tk.Button(control_panel, text="Open Video", command=self.open_video)
        self.open_button.grid(row=0, column=0, padx=10, pady=5)

        # Combobox for selecting zoom scale
        self.zoom_combobox = ttk.Combobox(control_panel, textvariable=self.zoom_scale, values=list(range(1, 11)))
        self.zoom_combobox.grid(row=0, column=1, padx=10, pady=5)
        self.zoom_combobox.bind("<<ComboboxSelected>>", self.update_zoom)

        # Button to play/pause the video
        self.play_button = tk.Button(control_panel, text="Play/Pause", command=self.toggle_play_pause)
        self.play_button.grid(row=0, column=2, padx=10, pady=5)

        # Button to stop the video
        self.stop_button = tk.Button(control_panel, text="Stop", command=self.stop_video)
        self.stop_button.grid(row=0, column=3, padx=10, pady=5)

        # Button to navigate to the previous frame
        self.prev_frame_button = tk.Button(control_panel, text="Previous Frame", command=self.prev_frame)
        self.prev_frame_button.grid(row=0, column=4, padx=10, pady=5)

        # Button to navigate to the next frame
```

```python
        self.next_frame_button = tk.Button(control_panel, text="Next Frame", command=self.next_frame)
        self.next_frame_button.grid(row=0, column=5, padx=10, pady=5)

        # Button to clear the listbox
        self.clear_button = tk.Button(control_panel, text="Clear Listbox", command=self.clear_listbox)
        self.clear_button.grid(row=0, column=6, padx=10, pady=5)

    def open_video(self):
        self.video_path = filedialog.askopenfilename(filetypes=[("Video files", "*.mp4;*.avi;*.mkv;*.wmv")])
        if self.video_path:
            self.video = imageio.get_reader(self.video_path)
            self.file_name = self.video_path.split('/')[-1]
            self.set_window_title()
            self.play_video()

    def play_video(self):
        if self.video:
            self.paused = False
            self.tracking_started = True
            self.show_frame()

    def stop_video(self):
        self.paused = True
        self.frame_index = 0
        self.bbox = None
        self.show_frame()

    def toggle_play_pause(self):
        self.paused = not self.paused
        if not self.paused:
            if self.bbox is not None:
                self.tracking_started = True
            self.play_video()

    def update_zoom(self, event=None):
        self.show_frame()

    def sift_vectors(self, prev_frame_gray, frame_gray):
        sift = cv2.xfeatures2d.SIFT_create()
        keypoints_prev, descriptors_prev = sift.detectAndCompute(prev_frame_gray, None)
        keypoints_frame, descriptors_frame = sift.detectAndCompute(frame_gray, None)

        # Create BFMatcher object
        bf = cv2.BFMatcher()
```

```python
        # Match descriptors
        matches = bf.knnMatch(descriptors_prev, descriptors_frame, k=2)

        # Apply ratio test
        good_matches = []
        for m, n in matches:
            if m.distance < 0.75 * n.distance:
                good_matches.append(m)

        # Check if there are enough good matches
        if len(good_matches) < 2:
            return np.zeros((1, 2))  # Return zero motion vector if there are not enough good matches

        # Estimate motion vectors from good matches
        motion_vectors = np.zeros((len(good_matches), 2))
        for i, match in enumerate(good_matches):
            # Get the keypoints for the matched points
            prev_point = keypoints_prev[match.queryIdx].pt
            frame_point = keypoints_frame[match.trainIdx].pt

            # Calculate the motion vector
            dx = frame_point[0] - prev_point[0]
            dy = frame_point[1] - prev_point[1]

            # Store the motion vector
            motion_vectors[i] = [dx, dy]

        return motion_vectors

    def track_object(self, frame, bbox):
        if bbox:
            x1, y1, x2, y2 = map(int, bbox)
            roi = frame[y1:y2, x1:x2]
            if roi.size > 0:
                # Convert the ROI to grayscale
                roi_gray = cv2.cvtColor(roi, cv2.COLOR_BGR2GRAY)
                # Initialize the previous frame if not already initialized or if its dimensions don't match the current frame
                if self.prev_frame_gray is None or self.prev_frame_gray.shape != roi_gray.shape:
                    self.prev_frame_gray = roi_gray.copy()

                # Calculate motion vectors using SIFT Algorithm
                motion_vectors = self.sift_vectors(self.prev_frame_gray, roi_gray)

                # Calculate the mean motion vector within the bounding box
```

```python
                mean_motion_vector = np.mean(motion_vectors, axis=0)

                # Update the bounding box coordinates based on the mean motion vector
                x1 += int(mean_motion_vector[0])
                y1 += int(mean_motion_vector[1])
                x2 += int(mean_motion_vector[0])
                y2 += int(mean_motion_vector[1])

                # Update the previous frame
                self.prev_frame_gray = roi_gray.copy()

                # Calculate the center of the bounding box
                center_x = (x1 + x2) // 2
                center_y = (y1 + y2) // 2

                # Add the center coordinates to the list box
                self.center_listbox.insert(tk.END, f"(center_x = {center_x}, center_y = {center_y})")

                return x1, y1, x2, y2
        return None

    def update_bbox_rectangle(self, bbox):
        if bbox is not None:
            x1, y1, x2, y2 = map(int, bbox)
            if self.bbox_rect is not None:
                self.canvas.coords(self.bbox_rect, x1, y1, x2, y2)
                self.canvas.tag_raise(self.bbox_rect)  # Raise the bounding box to the front
            else:
                self.bbox_rect = self.canvas.create_rectangle(x1, y1, x2-50, y2-50, outline='#fc3d3d', width=8, tags="bbox")

    def show_frame(self):
        if self.video:
            if not self.paused:
                if 0 <= self.frame_index < len(self.video):
                    if not self.frame_processing:  # Check if the frame is already being processed
                        try:
                            self.frame_processing = True  # Set frame_processing flag to True to indicate frame processing

                            frame = self.video.get_data(self.frame_index)
                            frame = cv2.cvtColor(frame, cv2.COLOR_RGB2BGR)

                            if self.bbox is not None:
                                if not self.tracking_started:
```

```python
                        self.tracking_started = True

                    self.bbox = self.track_object(frame, self.bbox)
                    if self.bbox:
                        frame = cv2.cvtColor(frame, cv2.COLOR_BGR2RGB)
                        frame = Image.fromarray(frame)
                        frame = frame.resize((frame.width * 
self.zoom_scale.get(), frame.height * self.zoom_scale.get()))
                        photo = ImageTk.PhotoImage(frame)
                        self.photo = photo
                        self.canvas.delete("video")
                        self.canvas.create_image(0, 0, anchor="nw", 
image=photo, tags="video")

                        self.update_bbox_rectangle(self.bbox)

                    else:
                        frame = cv2.cvtColor(frame, cv2.COLOR_BGR2RGB)
                        frame = Image.fromarray(frame)
                        frame = frame.resize((frame.width * 
self.zoom_scale.get(), frame.height * self.zoom_scale.get()))
                        photo = ImageTk.PhotoImage(frame)
                        self.photo = photo
                        self.canvas.delete("video")
                        self.canvas.create_image(0, 0, anchor="nw", 
image=photo, tags="video")

                    self.frame_number_label.config(text=f"Frame: 
{self.frame_index} / {self.video.count_frames()}", font=("Helvetica", 18))

                    self.frame_index += 1

            except Exception as e:
                print("Error: ", e)
            finally:
                self.frame_processing = False  # Reset frame_processing 
flag to False after processing the frame

    def on_mousewheel(self, event):
        direction = event.delta // 120
        current_value = int(self.zoom_scale.get())
        if direction == 1 and current_value < 10:
            current_value += 1
        elif direction == -1 and current_value > 1:
            current_value -= 1
        self.zoom_scale.set(current_value)
        self.update_zoom()

    def on_press(self, event):
```

```python
        self.start_x = self.canvas.canvasx(event.x)
        self.start_y = self.canvas.canvasy(event.y)
        self.bbox = None

    def on_drag(self, event):
        cur_x = self.canvas.canvasx(event.x)
        cur_y = self.canvas.canvasy(event.y)
        if self.bbox_rect:
            self.canvas.delete(self.bbox_rect)
        self.bbox = (self.start_x, self.start_y, cur_x, cur_y)
        self.bbox_rect = self.canvas.create_rectangle(*self.bbox, outline='#fc3d3d', width=6)

    def prev_frame(self):
        if self.frame_index > 0:
            self.frame_index -= 1
            self.show_frame()

    def next_frame(self):
        if self.video and self.frame_index < len(self.video) - 1:
            self.show_frame()

    def clear_listbox(self):
        self.center_listbox.delete(0, tk.END)

    def set_window_title(self):
        if self.file_name:
            self.master.title(f"Object Tracking with SIFT Algorithm - {self.file_name}")
            self.master.title_font = ("Helvetica", 16, "bold")
        else:
            self.master.title("Object Tracking with SIFT Algorithm")

def main():
    root = tk.Tk()
    app = ObjectTrackingSIFT(root)
    root.mainloop()

if __name__ == "__main__":
    main()
```

OBJECT TRACKING WITH ORB (ORIENTED FAST AND ROTATED BRIEF)

DESCRIPTION

The purpose of the "Object Tracking with ORB (Oriented FAST and Rotated BRIEF)" project is to develop a graphical user interface (GUI) application for tracking objects within a video using the ORB algorithm. Here's a detailed explanation of its objectives:

The project aims to provide a user-friendly interface for tracking objects in videos. It utilizes the Tkinter library in Python to create a GUI application where users can interact with the video playback and object tracking functionalities.

One of the primary goals is to enable users to open video files of various formats (e.g., .mp4, .avi, .mkv) through a file dialog. This functionality allows users to select the video they want to analyze for object tracking.

The application facilitates video playback controls, including play/pause, stop, and navigation to previous and next frames. These controls enhance the user experience by providing flexibility in reviewing the video content frame by frame.

The zoom functionality allows users to adjust the scale of the video display, enabling closer examination of specific regions within the frames. This feature enhances precision in object tracking tasks by providing finer control over the displayed content.

The project integrates the ORB (Oriented FAST and Rotated BRIEF) algorithm for object tracking. ORB is a feature-based algorithm capable of detecting and describing keypoints in images, making it suitable for object recognition and tracking tasks.

The application utilizes the ORB algorithm to compute keypoints and descriptors for consecutive frames in the video. By matching descriptors between frames, the algorithm estimates motion vectors, enabling the tracking of objects across the video sequence.

A key objective of the project is to visualize the object tracking process in real-time within the GUI. The application displays the video frames with overlaid bounding boxes that track the detected objects. This visualization aids users in understanding the effectiveness of the tracking algorithm.

The project also includes features for user interaction, such as selecting regions of interest (ROIs) within frames for tracking. Users can define bounding boxes by clicking and dragging on the video canvas, enabling custom object tracking configurations.

Additionally, the application provides feedback on the tracking process by displaying the center coordinates of the bounding boxes in a listbox. This feedback mechanism allows users to monitor the movement of tracked objects throughout the video.

Overall, the "Object Tracking with ORB" project serves as a versatile tool for video analysis tasks, offering intuitive controls, real-time visualization of object tracking, and integration of the ORB algorithm for robust and efficient tracking performance.

TRACKING OBJECT

```python
def orb_vectors(self, prev_frame_gray, frame_gray):
    orb = cv2.ORB_create()
    keypoints_prev, descriptors_prev = orb.detectAndCompute(prev_frame_gray, None)
```

```python
            keypoints_frame, descriptors_frame = orb.detectAndCompute(frame_gray, None)

            # Create BFMatcher object
            bf = cv2.BFMatcher(cv2.NORM_HAMMING, crossCheck=True)

            # Match descriptors
            matches = bf.match(descriptors_prev, descriptors_frame)

            # Check if there are matches
            if len(matches) == 0:
                return np.zeros((1, 2))  # Return zero motion vector if no matches found

            # Estimate motion vectors from matches
            motion_vectors = np.zeros((len(matches), 2))
            for i, match in enumerate(matches):
                # Get the keypoints for the matched points
                prev_point = keypoints_prev[match.queryIdx].pt
                frame_point = keypoints_frame[match.trainIdx].pt

                # Calculate the motion vector
                dx = frame_point[0] - prev_point[0]
                dy = frame_point[1] - prev_point[1]

                # Store the motion vector
                motion_vectors[i] = [dx, dy]

            return motion_vectors

    def track_object(self, frame, bbox):
        if bbox:
            x1, y1, x2, y2 = map(int, bbox)
            roi = frame[y1:y2, x1:x2]
            if roi.size > 0:
                # Convert the ROI to grayscale
                roi_gray = cv2.cvtColor(roi, cv2.COLOR_BGR2GRAY)
                # Initialize the previous frame if not already initialized or if its
dimensions don't match the current frame
                if self.prev_frame_gray is None or self.prev_frame_gray.shape != roi_gray.shape:
                    self.prev_frame_gray = roi_gray.copy()

                # Calculate motion vectors using ORB Algorithm
                motion_vectors = self.orb_vectors(self.prev_frame_gray, roi_gray)

                # Calculate the mean motion vector within the bounding box
                mean_motion_vector = np.mean(motion_vectors, axis=0)

                # Update the bounding box coordinates based on the mean motion vector
```

```
            x1 += int(mean_motion_vector[0])
            y1 += int(mean_motion_vector[1])
            x2 += int(mean_motion_vector[0])
            y2 += int(mean_motion_vector[1])

            # Update the previous frame
            self.prev_frame_gray = roi_gray.copy()

            # Calculate the center of the bounding box
            center_x = (x1 + x2) // 2
            center_y = (y1 + y2) // 2

            # Add the center coordinates to the list box
            self.center_listbox.insert(tk.END, f"(center_x = {center_x}, center_y = {center_y})")

            return x1, y1, x2, y2
        return None
```

The orb_vectors() method calculates the motion vectors between keypoints detected in consecutive frames using the ORB (Oriented FAST and Rotated BRIEF) algorithm. Here's how it works:

1. First, the method initializes an ORB detector using cv2.ORB_create(). This detector is capable of detecting keypoints and computing descriptors for the input grayscale images (prev_frame_gray and frame_gray).
2. Next, it computes keypoints and descriptors for both the previous and current frames using the ORB detector. These keypoints and descriptors represent distinctive features in the images that can be matched between frames to estimate motion.
3. Then, a Brute-Force Matcher (cv2.BFMatcher) is created to match descriptors between the previous and current frames. This matcher is configured to use the Hamming distance (cv2.NORM_HAMMING) and perform cross-checking (crossCheck=True) to improve matching accuracy.
4. The method matches descriptors between the previous and current frames using the Brute-Force Matcher. If no matches are found (i.e., if the length of the matches list is zero), it returns a zero motion vector indicating that no motion was detected.
5. If matches are found, the method estimates motion vectors for each match by subtracting the keypoint coordinates of the matched points between frames. These motion vectors represent the displacement of keypoints between frames.

6. Finally, the method returns an array containing the calculated motion vectors for all matches.

The track_object() method utilizes the orb_vectors() method to track an object within a bounding box (bbox) in a video frame. Here's a breakdown of its functionality:
1. First, it extracts the region of interest (ROI) from the input frame based on the provided bounding box coordinates (x1, y1, x2, y2).
2. If the ROI is valid (i.e., it contains image data), the method converts it to grayscale.
3. It then initializes the previous frame (prev_frame_gray) if it hasn't been initialized yet or if its dimensions don't match the current ROI.
4. Next, it calls the orb_vectors() method to calculate motion vectors within the ROI between the current and previous frames.
5. The method computes the mean motion vector from the calculated motion vectors, representing the average motion within the ROI.
6. Based on the mean motion vector, it updates the bounding box coordinates (x1, y1, x2, y2) to adjust the position of the tracked object in the current frame.
7. The previous frame is updated with the current ROI (roi_gray).
8. It calculates the center coordinates of the updated bounding box and adds them to a list box for visualization and tracking feedback.
9. Finally, it returns the updated bounding box coordinates, allowing the GUI application to display the tracked object in the video frame.
10. If the input bounding box is empty (i.e., bbox is None), indicating that no object is being tracked, the method returns None.

RUNNING PROGRAM

Run program and click on Open Video button. Then, choose a video file then click on Next Frame button.

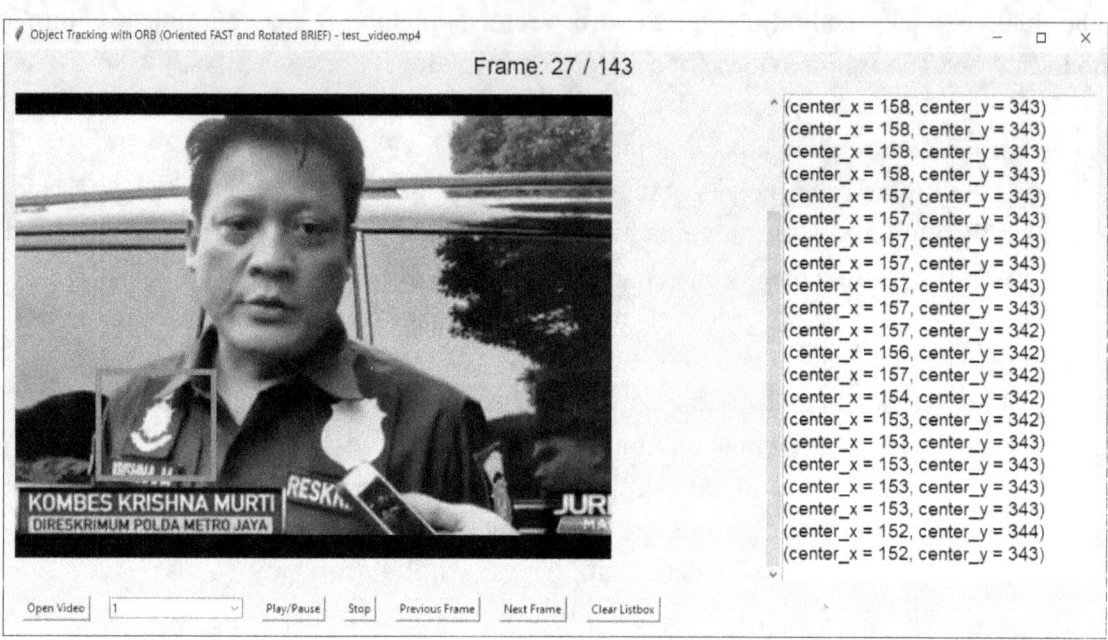

SOURCE CODE

```python
# object_tracking_orb.py
import tkinter as tk
from tkinter import ttk
from tkinter import filedialog
from PIL import Image, ImageTk
import imageio
import cv2
import numpy as np

class ObjectTracking_ORB:
    def __init__(self, master):
        self.master = master
        self.master.title("Object Tracking with ORB (Oriented FAST and Rotated BRIEF)")
        self.file_name = ""
        self.set_window_title()  # Set window title initially

        self.frame_number_label = tk.Label(master, text="Frame: 0")
        self.frame_number_label.pack()

        self.video = None
        self.video_path = None
        self.paused = False
```

```python
        self.zoom_scale = tk.IntVar(value=1)
        self.frame_index = 0
        self.bbox = None
        self.tracking_started = False  # Initialize tracking_started to False
        self.prev_frame_gray = None

        self.bbox_rect = None  # Initialize bbox_rect attribute to None
        self.frame_processing = False  # Initialize frame_processing attribute to False

        self.create_widgets()

    def create_widgets(self):
        # Panel for video display
        video_panel = tk.Frame(self.master)
        video_panel.pack(padx=10, pady=10)

        # Canvas to display the original video
        canvas_width = 800
        canvas_height = 500
        self.canvas = tk.Canvas(video_panel, width=canvas_width, height=canvas_height)
        self.canvas.pack(side="left", fill="both", expand=True)
        self.canvas.bind("<MouseWheel>", self.on_mousewheel)
        self.canvas.bind("<ButtonPress-1>", self.on_press)
        self.canvas.bind("<B1-Motion>", self.on_drag)

        # List box to display center coordinates
        self.center_listbox = tk.Listbox(video_panel, width=30, height=20, font=("Helvetica", 14))
        self.center_listbox.pack(side="right", fill="y")
        # Scrollbar for the listbox
        scrollbar = tk.Scrollbar(video_panel, orient="vertical")
        scrollbar.pack(side="left", fill="y")
        scrollbar.config(command=self.center_listbox.yview)

        # Attach scrollbar to listbox
        self.center_listbox.config(yscrollcommand=scrollbar.set)

        # Panel for control buttons
        control_panel = tk.Frame(self.master)
        control_panel.pack(padx=10, pady=(0, 10), fill="x")

        # Button to open a video file
        self.open_button = tk.Button(control_panel, text="Open Video", command=self.open_video)
        self.open_button.grid(row=0, column=0, padx=10, pady=5)
```

```python
        # Combobox for selecting zoom scale
        self.zoom_combobox = ttk.Combobox(control_panel, 
textvariable=self.zoom_scale, values=list(range(1, 11)))
        self.zoom_combobox.grid(row=0, column=1, padx=10, pady=5)
        self.zoom_combobox.bind("<<ComboboxSelected>>", self.update_zoom)

        # Button to play/pause the video
        self.play_button = tk.Button(control_panel, text="Play/Pause", 
command=self.toggle_play_pause)
        self.play_button.grid(row=0, column=2, padx=10, pady=5)

        # Button to stop the video
        self.stop_button = tk.Button(control_panel, text="Stop", 
command=self.stop_video)
        self.stop_button.grid(row=0, column=3, padx=10, pady=5)

        # Button to navigate to the previous frame
        self.prev_frame_button = tk.Button(control_panel, text="Previous Frame", 
command=self.prev_frame)
        self.prev_frame_button.grid(row=0, column=4, padx=10, pady=5)

        # Button to navigate to the next frame
        self.next_frame_button = tk.Button(control_panel, text="Next Frame", 
command=self.next_frame)
        self.next_frame_button.grid(row=0, column=5, padx=10, pady=5)

        # Button to clear the listbox
        self.clear_button = tk.Button(control_panel, text="Clear Listbox", 
command=self.clear_listbox)
        self.clear_button.grid(row=0, column=6, padx=10, pady=5)

    def open_video(self):
        self.video_path = filedialog.askopenfilename(filetypes=[("Video files", 
"*.mp4;*.avi;*.mkv;*.wmv")])
        if self.video_path:
            self.video = imageio.get_reader(self.video_path)
            self.file_name = self.video_path.split('/')[-1]
            self.set_window_title()
            self.play_video()

    def play_video(self):
        if self.video:
            self.paused = False
            self.tracking_started = True
            self.show_frame()

    def stop_video(self):
        self.paused = True
```

```python
        self.frame_index = 0
        self.bbox = None
        self.show_frame()

    def toggle_play_pause(self):
        self.paused = not self.paused
        if not self.paused:
            if self.bbox is not None:
                self.tracking_started = True
            self.play_video()

    def update_zoom(self, event=None):
        self.show_frame()

    def orb_vectors(self, prev_frame_gray, frame_gray):
        orb = cv2.ORB_create()
        keypoints_prev, descriptors_prev = orb.detectAndCompute(prev_frame_gray, None)
        keypoints_frame, descriptors_frame = orb.detectAndCompute(frame_gray, None)

        # Create BFMatcher object
        bf = cv2.BFMatcher(cv2.NORM_HAMMING, crossCheck=True)

        # Match descriptors
        matches = bf.match(descriptors_prev, descriptors_frame)

        # Check if there are matches
        if len(matches) == 0:
            return np.zeros((1, 2))  # Return zero motion vector if no matches found

        # Estimate motion vectors from matches
        motion_vectors = np.zeros((len(matches), 2))
        for i, match in enumerate(matches):
            # Get the keypoints for the matched points
            prev_point = keypoints_prev[match.queryIdx].pt
            frame_point = keypoints_frame[match.trainIdx].pt

            # Calculate the motion vector
            dx = frame_point[0] - prev_point[0]
            dy = frame_point[1] - prev_point[1]

            # Store the motion vector
            motion_vectors[i] = [dx, dy]

        return motion_vectors

    def track_object(self, frame, bbox):
        if bbox:
```

```python
            x1, y1, x2, y2 = map(int, bbox)
            roi = frame[y1:y2, x1:x2]
            if roi.size > 0:
                # Convert the ROI to grayscale
                roi_gray = cv2.cvtColor(roi, cv2.COLOR_BGR2GRAY)
                # Initialize the previous frame if not already initialized or if its dimensions don't match the current frame
                if self.prev_frame_gray is None or self.prev_frame_gray.shape != roi_gray.shape:
                    self.prev_frame_gray = roi_gray.copy()

                # Calculate motion vectors using ORB Algorithm
                motion_vectors = self.orb_vectors(self.prev_frame_gray, roi_gray)

                # Calculate the mean motion vector within the bounding box
                mean_motion_vector = np.mean(motion_vectors, axis=0)

                # Update the bounding box coordinates based on the mean motion vector
                x1 += int(mean_motion_vector[0])
                y1 += int(mean_motion_vector[1])
                x2 += int(mean_motion_vector[0])
                y2 += int(mean_motion_vector[1])

                # Update the previous frame
                self.prev_frame_gray = roi_gray.copy()

                # Calculate the center of the bounding box
                center_x = (x1 + x2) // 2
                center_y = (y1 + y2) // 2

                # Add the center coordinates to the list box
                self.center_listbox.insert(tk.END, f"(center_x = {center_x}, center_y = {center_y})")

                return x1, y1, x2, y2
        return None

    def update_bbox_rectangle(self, bbox):
        if bbox is not None:
            x1, y1, x2, y2 = map(int, bbox)
            if self.bbox_rect is not None:
                self.canvas.coords(self.bbox_rect, x1, y1, x2, y2)
                self.canvas.tag_raise(self.bbox_rect)  # Raise the bounding box to the front
            else:
                self.bbox_rect = self.canvas.create_rectangle(x1, y1, x2-50, y2-50, outline='#fc3d3d', width=8, tags="bbox")
```

```python
    def show_frame(self):
        if self.video:
            if not self.paused:
                if 0 <= self.frame_index < len(self.video):
                    if not self.frame_processing:  # Check if the frame is already being processed
                        try:
                            self.frame_processing = True  # Set frame_processing flag to True to indicate frame processing

                            frame = self.video.get_data(self.frame_index)
                            frame = cv2.cvtColor(frame, cv2.COLOR_RGB2BGR)

                            if self.bbox is not None:
                                if not self.tracking_started:
                                    self.tracking_started = True

                                self.bbox = self.track_object(frame, self.bbox)
                                if self.bbox:
                                    frame = cv2.cvtColor(frame, cv2.COLOR_BGR2RGB)
                                    frame = Image.fromarray(frame)
                                    frame = frame.resize((frame.width * self.zoom_scale.get(), frame.height * self.zoom_scale.get()))
                                    photo = ImageTk.PhotoImage(frame)
                                    self.photo = photo
                                    self.canvas.delete("video")
                                    self.canvas.create_image(0, 0, anchor="nw", image=photo, tags="video")

                                    self.update_bbox_rectangle(self.bbox)

                            else:
                                frame = cv2.cvtColor(frame, cv2.COLOR_BGR2RGB)
                                frame = Image.fromarray(frame)
                                frame = frame.resize((frame.width * self.zoom_scale.get(), frame.height * self.zoom_scale.get()))
                                photo = ImageTk.PhotoImage(frame)
                                self.photo = photo
                                self.canvas.delete("video")
                                self.canvas.create_image(0, 0, anchor="nw", image=photo, tags="video")

                            self.frame_number_label.config(text=f"Frame: {self.frame_index} / {self.video.count_frames()}", font=("Helvetica", 18))

                            self.frame_index += 1

                        except Exception as e:
                            print("Error: ", e)
```

```python
            finally:
                self.frame_processing = False  # Reset frame_processing flag to False after processing the frame

    def on_mousewheel(self, event):
        direction = event.delta // 120
        current_value = int(self.zoom_scale.get())
        if direction == 1 and current_value < 10:
            current_value += 1
        elif direction == -1 and current_value > 1:
            current_value -= 1
        self.zoom_scale.set(current_value)
        self.update_zoom()

    def on_press(self, event):
        self.start_x = self.canvas.canvasx(event.x)
        self.start_y = self.canvas.canvasy(event.y)
        self.bbox = None

    def on_drag(self, event):
        cur_x = self.canvas.canvasx(event.x)
        cur_y = self.canvas.canvasy(event.y)
        if self.bbox_rect:
            self.canvas.delete(self.bbox_rect)
        self.bbox = (self.start_x, self.start_y, cur_x, cur_y)
        self.bbox_rect = self.canvas.create_rectangle(*self.bbox, outline='#fc3d3d', width=6)

    def prev_frame(self):
        if self.frame_index > 0:
            self.frame_index -= 1
            self.show_frame()

    def next_frame(self):
        if self.video and self.frame_index < len(self.video) - 1:
            self.show_frame()

    def clear_listbox(self):
        self.center_listbox.delete(0, tk.END)

    def set_window_title(self):
        if self.file_name:
            self.master.title(f"Object Tracking with ORB (Oriented FAST and Rotated BRIEF) - {self.file_name}")
            self.master.title_font = ("Helvetica", 16, "bold")
        else:
            self.master.title("Object Tracking with ORB (Oriented FAST and Rotated BRIEF)")
```

```
def main():
    root = tk.Tk()
    app = ObjectTracking_ORB(root)
    root.mainloop()

if __name__ == "__main__":
    main()
```

Bibliography

Vivian Siahaan and Rismon Hasiholan Sianipar. *TKINTER, DATA SCIENCE, AND MACHINE LEARNING*. North Sumatera: Balige Publishing, 2023.

Vivian Siahaan and Rismon Hasiholan Sianipar. *DATA VISUALIZATION, TIME-SERIES FORECASTING, AND PREDICTION USING MACHINE LEARNING WITH TKINTER*. North Sumatera: Balige Publishing, 2023.

Vivian Siahaan and Rismon Hasiholan Sianipar. *TIME-SERIES WEATHER FORECASTING AND PREDICTION USING MACHINE LEARNING WITH TKINTER*. North Sumatera: Balige Publishing, 2023.

Vivian Siahaan and Rismon Hasiholan Sianipar. DATA VISUALIZATION, TIME-SERIES FORECASTING, AND PREDICTION USING MACHINE LEARNING WITH TKINTER. North Sumatera: Balige Publishing, 2023.

Vivian Siahaan and Rismon Hasiholan Sianipar. START FROM SCRATCH DIGITAL SIGNAL PROCESSING WITH TKINTER. North Sumatera: Balige Publishing, 2023.

Vivian Siahaan and Rismon Hasiholan Sianipar. START FROM SCRATCH DIGITAL IMAGE PROCESSING WITH TKINTER. North Sumatera: Balige Publishing, 2023.

Vivian Siahaan and Rismon Hasiholan Sianipar. START FROM SCRATCH DIGITAL IMAGE PROCESSING WITH TKINTER. North Sumatera: Balige Publishing, 2023.

Vivian Siahaan and Rismon Hasiholan Sianipar. IMAGE DENOISING, EDGE DETECTION, AND SEGMENTATION WITH TKINTER. North Sumatera: Balige Publishing, 2023.

Vivian Siahaan and Rismon Hasiholan Sianipar. DIGITAL VIDEO PROCESSING PROJECTS USING PYTHON AND TKINTER. North Sumatera: Balige Publishing, 2024.

Vivian Siahaan and Rismon Hasiholan Sianipar. FRAME ANALYSIS AND PROCESSING IN DIGITAL VIDEO USING PYTHON AND TKINTER. North Sumatera: Balige Publishing, 2024.

Vivian Siahaan and Rismon Hasiholan Sianipar. MOTION ANALYSIS AND OBJECT TRACKING USING PYTHON AND TKINTER. North Sumatera: Balige Publishing, 2024.

Vivian Siahaan and Rismon Hasiholan Sianipar. FRAME FILTERING AND EDGES-DETECTION USING PYTHON AND TKINTER. North Sumatera: Balige Publishing, 2024.

Vivian Siahaan and Rismon Hasiholan Sianipar. OPTICAL FLOW ANALYSIS AND MOTION ESTIMATION IN DIGITAL VIDEO WITH PYTHON AND TKINTER. North Sumatera: Balige Publishing, 2024.

www.ingramcontent.com/pod-product-compliance
Lightning Source LLC
Chambersburg PA
CBHW062103220526
45471CB00010B/3580